Improving Development Teams Support Deliberate Developmen Air Force Officers

Lawrence M. Hanser, Nelson Lim, Douglas Yeung, Eric Cring

RAND Project AIR FORCE

Prepared for the United States Air Force
Approved for public release; distribution unlimited

For more information on this publication, visit www.rand.org/t/RR1010

Library of Congress Cataloging-in-Publication Data is available for this publication.

ISBN: 978-0-8330-9013-3

Published by the RAND Corporation, Santa Monica, Calif.

© Copyright 2015 RAND Corporation

RAND® is a registered trademark.

Limited Print and Electronic Distribution Rights

This document and trademark(s) contained herein are protected by law. This representation of RAND intellectual property is provided for noncommercial use only. Unauthorized posting of this publication online is prohibited. Permission is given to duplicate this document for personal use only, as long as it is unaltered and complete. Permission is required from RAND to reproduce, or reuse in another form, any of its research documents for commercial use. For information on reprint and linking permissions, please visit www.rand.org/pubs/permissions.html.

The RAND Corporation is a research organization that develops solutions to public policy challenges to help make communities throughout the world safer and more secure, healthier and more prosperous. RAND is nonprofit, nonpartisan, and committed to the public interest.

RAND's publications do not necessarily reflect the opinions of its research clients and sponsors.

Support RAND
Make a tax-deductible charitable contribution at
www.rand.org/giving/contribute

www.rand.org

Preface

Newly commissioned Air Force officers mature into midlevel and senior leaders by gaining experience throughout their careers through assignments to positions of increasing responsibility and participation in a number of developmental education opportunities. Prior to 2004, officer development hinged primarily on trained assignment teams at the Air Force Personnel Center led by a more-senior officer from the relevant career field and each officer's individual understanding—and the understanding of the officer's mentor—of what was required to progress as an Air Force officer. The Air Force Personnel Center manages the actual scheduling of professional military education attendance and assignments. A new concept of leadership and force development, including the implementation of development teams (DTs), was initially briefed to the Corona meeting of Air Force four-star generals and other senior leaders in September 2002 and published as Air Force doctrine in February 2004. In 2013, after nearly nine years of experience with DTs, Air Force leadership asked for a review of the role of DTs in the force development construct. This research addresses the questions of whether DTs should continue to operate and, if so, how.

This report should be of interest to senior Air Force leaders who bear direct or indirect responsibility for developing the waves of officers who will succeed them as Air Force leaders and to all Air Force officers who envision continuing their careers as Air Force officers. Related RAND Project AIR FORCE work includes the following:

- *Advancing the U.S. Air Force's Force-Development Initiative* (Moore and Brauner, 2007)
- *Human Capital Management for the USAF Cyber Force* (Scott et al., 2010)
- *Understrength Air Force Officer Career Fields: A Force Management Approach* (Galway et al., 2005)
- *Sustaining the U.S. Air Force's Force Support Career Field Through Officer Workforce Planning* (O'Neill, 2012).

The research reported here was sponsored by the Air Force Deputy Chief of Staff for Manpower, Personnel and Services (AF/A1) and conducted within the Manpower, Personnel, and Training Program of RAND Project AIR FORCE.

RAND Project AIR FORCE

RAND Project AIR FORCE (PAF), a division of the RAND Corporation, is the U.S. Air Force's federally funded research and development center for studies and analyses. PAF provides the Air Force with independent analyses of policy alternatives affecting the development, employment, combat readiness, and support of current and future air, space, and cyber forces. Research is conducted in four programs: Force Modernization and Employment;

Manpower, Personnel, and Training; Resource Management; and Strategy and Doctrine. The research reported here was prepared under contract FA7014-06-C-0001.

Additional information about PAF is available on our website at:
http://www.rand.org/paf

Table of Contents

Appendixes

Figures and Tables

Figures

Tables

Summary

A new concept for leadership and force development was initially proposed at the Corona meeting of Air Force four-star generals and other senior leaders in September 2002 and was promulgated as Air Force Doctrine Document (AFDD) 1-1, *Leadership and Force Development*, in February 2004. This new concept included the implementation of development teams (DTs), which have since played a critical role in the Air Force's force development system.

Air Force Instruction (AFI) 36-2640, *Executing Total Force Development*, states that the primary function of DTs is "to be the conduit between the force development systems, frameworks and policy and translate these into career vectors," individualized career paths consisting of recommended assignments appropriate for officer development. To perform this function, DTs require considerable personnel and financial support. DT members include a general officer as chair, a career field manager, an assignment team representative, and other senior officer (or civilian equivalent) stakeholders from the Air Staff or major command headquarters. In fiscal year 2012, there were 28 DTs, each of which met approximately twice per year.

After nearly nine years of experience with DTs, Air Force senior leaders raised questions about their value in the force development process. A rigorous examination of DTs is also warranted in the emerging austere budget environment, to find ways to improve DTs' efficiency and effectiveness. Responding to Air Force senior leaders' questions and concerns about the value of DTs, a RAND research team conducted a comprehensive examination of DTs and how they affect the force development system.

The Origin of Development Teams

The current force development system, in which the DTs play a key role, was developed in 2002 to allay concerns about how to best develop individual officers while serving the overall interests of the Air Force. In September 2002, the director of the Air Force Senior Leader Management Office briefed Corona on a new plan for force development (Hassan, 2002). He contrasted the existing force development system, which he said depended on "chance," with a more systematic, deliberate approach. He said that "career stovepipes" were the dominant situation, meaning that officers built skills and competencies only within their chosen career fields. The Air Force, he argued, needed to build wider perspectives, including a force development system that would develop skills that were more broadly applicable skills, rather than just job specific.

Preparing officers of the future to meet the needs of the Air Force would entail creating a simple, understandable, deliberate development system for the warfighter that

- satisfied necessary skill and enduring competency needs
- followed doctrine
- had coordinated policies that concentrate on the right level and focus on experience, education, and training at the right time
- best utilized available time for force development.

The focus of development was to be on individuals, balanced with Air Force needs.

Operationalizing development was intended to have two key elements. First, an individualized plan would serve as a modifiable, updatable, "living" document of near- and far-term goals and objectives. This plan would be built collaboratively by the officer, his or her supervisor or squadron commander, and a professional development team (what is now known as the DT), with the Air Force Personnel Center (AFPC) acting as a consult and requirements broker. The DT team was the second key element of the proposal to operationalize development. The DT would meet semiannually to review officers' plans and performance assessments from supervisors or squadron commanders (and sometimes senior raters). The process would be timed appropriately for education or special duties and would ensure that the needs of the Air Force were met. Finally, the DT would provide feedback to both the officer and his or her supervisor or squadron commander. This feedback was intended to close the loop between officer and commander for the first time.

Current Development Team Practices[1]

In interviews, DT chairs generally stated similar objectives, such as developing leaders to fulfill career field needs and to achieve the Air Force mission, but they differed on a wide range of dimensions relating to how to achieve these goals. Most DT chairs explicitly mentioned that their goals were broad: to manage and grow the entire force. These multifaceted roles and obligations require DTs to find a way to balance Department of Defense, corporate Air Force, career field, and individual needs.

Guiding policy documents suggest that DTs perform four specific tasks:

1. Provide general guidance to the assignment team regarding future assignments for each officer ("steady-state vectoring").
2. Create a list of officers eligible to be selected for squadron command positions
3. Manage developmental education (DE) timing and school assignment for officers a central selection board has selected for in-residence schooling and for officers the DT has selected for in-residence schooling.
4. Provide feedback to officers.

---

[1] DT practices and the vocabulary describing them in this document were current when the research was undertaken. For example, as of the date of this publication, *steady-state vectoring* is now referred to as *developmental vectoring*. Furthermore, the recommendations in this report were widely discussed with Air Force policymakers at the time, and some policies current at the time of this research were changed as a result of these recommendations.

Providing Steady-State Vectoring

Official guidance says that DTs should vector—that is, provide DE and follow-on position recommendations for which individuals should be considered—the highest-quality officers for assignments that meet the needs of the Air Force but also provide appropriate career incentives. The point of the vectors is to provide officers and AFPC officer assignment teams with recommended future assignments designed to provide the officer with appropriate professional development, breadth, and knowledge within the Air Force.

Managing Developmental Education

Official guidance for force development states that DTs should manage education for the purpose of developing officers for the corporate and functional Air Force (e.g., Air Force Policy Directive 36-26, AFI 36-2640). Other official guidance states that "education deferments may be waived when they do not serve the overall best interest of the AF" (AFI 36-2110, 2009, p. 40). Annually updated guidance from AF/A1 reminds the DTs of the importance of DE and identifies high-priority areas for education and assignments. AFPC briefings at annual DT meetings also outline the DTs' role in nominating individuals for DE programs.

DT chairs said that, in selecting officers for DE opportunities, DTs intend to ensure that each officer receives appropriate training, jobs, or experience.

Providing Feedback to Officers

Recent examples of the annual guidance memorandums from the Air Force Deputy Chief of Staff for Manpower, Personnel, and Services (AF/A1) require the DTs to provide generalized feedback to officers. In addition, AFI 36-2640 states that DTs should provide feedback to career field managers to update career field pyramids, as well as "aggregate feedback" to officers and civilians, with senior raters to have primary responsibility for providing mentoring and feedback to individuals. More-detailed guidance to DTs regarding feedback is provided at the tactical level, emphasizing personalized, concrete feedback.

Our interviews with DT chairs suggest that feedback to the field varies widely, with some DTs emailing individuals directly or providing broader feedback through webinars or in the DT minutes. Several DT chairs suggested that they expected individual feedback to officers to come primarily from their commanders or through their chains of command.

Creating Command Lists

Strategic guidance states that the overarching goal of promotions is to further the objectives of the Air Force, promoting officers who are "fully qualified and best qualified to meet the prescribed needs of the Air Force" (AFI 36-2501, p. 13). The stated primary criterion for an assignment (AFI 36-2110) or for promotion to general officer (AFI 36-2501) would be the individual with the best qualifications (that is, the most qualified officer), implying that such factors as career field health do not play a role in the creation of command lists.

Several DT chairs agreed that the responsibility for picking commanders was properly situated with DTs, and exercising command list flexibility was seen as a particular strength of DTs.

Recommendations

To reform the DTs in ways that help foster deliberate force development and balance the interests of Air Force stakeholders, we provide nine recommendations, grouped topically. The details of these recommendations are provided in the body of the report:

- steady-state vectoring
  - DTs should no longer be required to provide steady-state vectors for all officers under review but should continue to vector and begin to track the progress of high-potential officers.
- managing developmental education
  - School seats should be allocated to DTs to meet requirements for the number of lieutenant colonels and colonels needed to fill positions in each career field.
  - The Air Force should implement several changes to the selection of officers for in-residence DE.
  - The Air Force should change how decisions are made about small-school attendees.
  - The Air Force should make school assignments in such a way that officers a central selection board school selects attend school as early as possible.
- providing feedback to officers
  - DTs should provide personalized, in addition to career field–wide, feedback to officers.
  - DTs should emphasize learning and development in their personalized feedback.
- creating command lists
  - The process for managing command lists should be standardized such that DTs provide multiple options for both officers and jobs to avoid pigeonholing officers and jobs.
- strategic objectives for DTs
  - All DTs should identify high-potential officers, chart out their recommended paths for development, and track the officer's progress.

The engagement of senior leaders from each career field in developing their field grade officers has a number of positive benefits that have convinced us to recommend that DTs continue into the future, with the modifications we have recommended above. The major benefit we see in the DT system is that it requires a broad swath of each career field's senior leaders to take stock of the status of their career field—not just the number of personnel in the pipeline but also their quality and the development needs of the career field and of the individuals in it. With this knowledge in hand, the DTs proceed to make decisions about and provide directions for the development of career field members.

Acknowledgments

The authors wish to thank Lt Gen Darrell D. Jones (ret.), then AF/A1, for his overall support and guidance throughout this project and for his review of this report. Regular conversations with Russell J. Frasz, AF/A1D, and analytic support from John Crown at AFPC and RAND colleagues Paul Emslie and Michael Schiefer helped to guide our deliberations. AF/A1D staff members Chanelle Johnson and William Hampton assisted with scheduling meetings with DT chairs and other administrative details. Finally, regular and lengthy meetings with General Jones that included Mr. Frasz; Maj Gen Alfred J. Stewart, AFPC/CC; Brig Gen Gina M. Grosso, AF/A1P; Robert E. Corsi, Deputy AF/A1; Barbara J. Barger, Deputy AF/A1D; and Todd A. Fore and John Crown, AFPC, helped fine tune both our observations and recommendations. We wish also to thank the DT chairs and AFPC staff who took time from their busy schedules to have thoughtful discussions about DT operations with us. In addition, Lisa Harrington and Shirley Ross provided pointed but helpful reviews of this report.

Abbreviations

AAD	advanced academic degree
ACSC	Air Command and Staff College
ADP	Airman Development Plan
AF	Air Force
AF/A1	Air Force Deputy Chief of Staff for Manpower, Personnel, and Services
AFA	Air Force Academy
AFDD	Air Force Decision Directive
AFERB	Air Force Education Requirements Board
AFI	Air Force instruction
AFPC	Air Force Personnel Center
AFPD	Air Force Policy Directive
AWC	Air War College
CAF	combat air forces
CC	commander
CDE	civilian developmental education
CFM	career field manager
CFT	Career Field Team
CSAF	Chief of Staff of the Air Force
CSB	central selection board
CV	vice commander
DAF	Department of the Air Force
DE	developmental education
DEDB	Developmental Education Designation Board
DPA	Air Force Personnel Center, Directorate of Assignments
DPAPF	Air Force Personnel Center, Force Development and Developmental Education Branch
DT	development team
FM	functional manager
FY	fiscal year
IDE	intermediate developmental education
MAJCOM	major command
MyDP	My Development Plan
NLT	no later than
ODP	officer development plan
OPR	office of primary responsibility

PME	professional military education
SDE	senior developmental education
USAF	U.S. Air Force
USAFA	U.S. Air Force Academy

1. Introduction

Each year, the Air Force commissions approximately 4,000 new officers, primarily through the U.S. Air Force Academy (USAFA or AFA), Reserve Officer Training Corps programs at colleges and universities across the United States, and Officer Training School. These entering officers mature into midlevel and senior leaders by gaining experience throughout their careers by being assigned to positions of increasing responsibility and by participating in a number of educational opportunities, including Squadron Officer School and intermediate (IDE) and senior (SDE) developmental education (DE). The military services are unique in that all service members enter at the bottom and advance upward into positions with increasing levels of responsibility and more-strategic leadership burdens. The result is that the organization itself must develop whatever knowledge, skill, or ability an officer will need at higher levels.[2]

The management of officer careers has been and continues to be an exercise in achieving a balance among the desires of each individual officer (e.g., assignment to a specific Air Force base or kind of position), the needs of the career field (e.g., assignments that provide officers with specific key occupation-specific experience), and the needs of the Air Force (e.g., to fill positions in less-desirable locations). Attendance at and choice of professional military education (PME) is also balanced against the needs and desires of individual officers, the career field, and the Air Force.

Prior to 2004, officer development hinged primarily on trained assignment teams at the Air Force Personnel Center (AFPC)—each led by a more-senior field-grade officer from the relevant career field and each officer's individual understanding—and the understanding of the officer's mentor—of what was required to progress as an Air Force officer. Assignment teams at AFPC consisted of officers from the career field they managed. These teams of young officers (typically captains or majors) were led by an experienced field-grade officer (typically a major or lieutenant colonel with over 14 years of military service). The purpose of the assignment teams was to manage individual careers while serving the needs of the Air Force. These two goals were not and are not mutually exclusive. Assignment teams were responsible for managing the career field and worked closely with the senior officers from that career field. Overseeing assignment teams was the AFPC Assignment Directorate, which was designed to have a better understanding of the bigger picture for balancing the needs of the Air Force with the desires of individual officers. At AFPC, a permanent staff of trained assignment officers led by a more-senior officer

---

[2] It also means that assignments are filled by a succession of officers. We specifically use the word *succession* because organizations that fill positions from within often engage in deliberate succession planning. Within the Air Force, most of the more-deliberate succession planning is for general officer positions (the top four ranks); not unexpectedly, succession planning tapers off dramatically for positions filled by officers below the top five ranks (i.e., below the rank of colonel).

managed the actual scheduling of attendance at professional military education and of assignments.

A new concept of leadership and force development was initially proposed at the Corona meeting of Air Force four-star generals and other senior leaders in September 2002 and was promulgated in Air Force Doctrine Document 1 (AFDD) 1-1, *Leadership and Force Development*, in February 2004. Key to this new concept of leadership and force development was the recognition that leadership at the "strategic level includes challenges to gain breadth of experience and leadership perspective (e.g., logical pairings of skills; educational opportunities, and training focused on the institutional Air Force; joint, intergovernment, business and international views)." That is, the new construct recognized that strategic leaders need to be competent and experienced more broadly than their own specific primary career field. Development teams (DTs) were created to implement the new force development construct and have since played a critical role in the Air Force's force development system.

In contrast to assignment teams, the DTs are large, ad hoc committees representing a single career field or cluster of related career fields. DT members have not been trained in force development processes and meet perhaps only twice a year, with turnover of some committee members year-to-year. As a result, although they may provide much greater senior representation and a broader and deeper understanding of the needs of a career field for development, their perspectives on development are likely to be viewed through the lens of their own experiences. Years of experience in the Air Force also differ between assignment teams and DTs. Assignment teams had (and still have) fewer and lower ranking members than DTs, whose membership consists of more senior and more experienced officers. For example, the combat air forces (CAF) DT held in 2010 was chaired by a brigadier general and had 22 colonels who were members, 15 of whom were then serving as commanders. In another example, the DT for intelligence officers (Air Force Specialty Code 14N), consisted of a brigadier general (chair) and ten colonels, four of whom were serving as commanders. As a result of the senior level of DT members and their representation of commands from across the Air Force, it is likely that one or more DT members know every officer whose records come before a DT for review personally.

Air Force Instruction (AFI) 36-2640, *Executing Total Force Development*, states that the primary function of DTs is "to be the conduit between the force development systems, frameworks and policy and translate these into career vectors," that is, into individualized career paths consisting of recommended assignments appropriate for officer development. To perform this function, DTs require considerable personnel and financial support. DT members include a general officer who chairs the team, a career field manager, an assignment team representative, and other senior officer (or civilian equivalent) stakeholders from the Air Staff and/or major command (MAJCOM) headquarters. In fiscal year (FY) 2012, there were 28 DTs, each of which met approximately twice per year.

Four Air Force Stakeholder Groups Have Different Interests and Time Horizons

A key challenge in deliberate force development is that different stakeholder groups also have different—in some cases, competing—interests. We identified four groups of stakeholders: (1) the corporate Air Force and joint community, (2) commanders, (3) functional communities, and (4) the individual officers (see Figure 1.1.). The corporate Air Force and the joint community have long-term development interests in maintaining a competent workforce, including developing all ranks of civilians, enlisted airmen, and officers, to have the right mix of skills to fulfill mission objectives. A high-level, competent workforce also implies the development, over time, of a large cadre of high-potential officers, some of whom will reach senior leadership

Figure 1.1. Stakeholders in the Deliberate Development of Air Force Officers

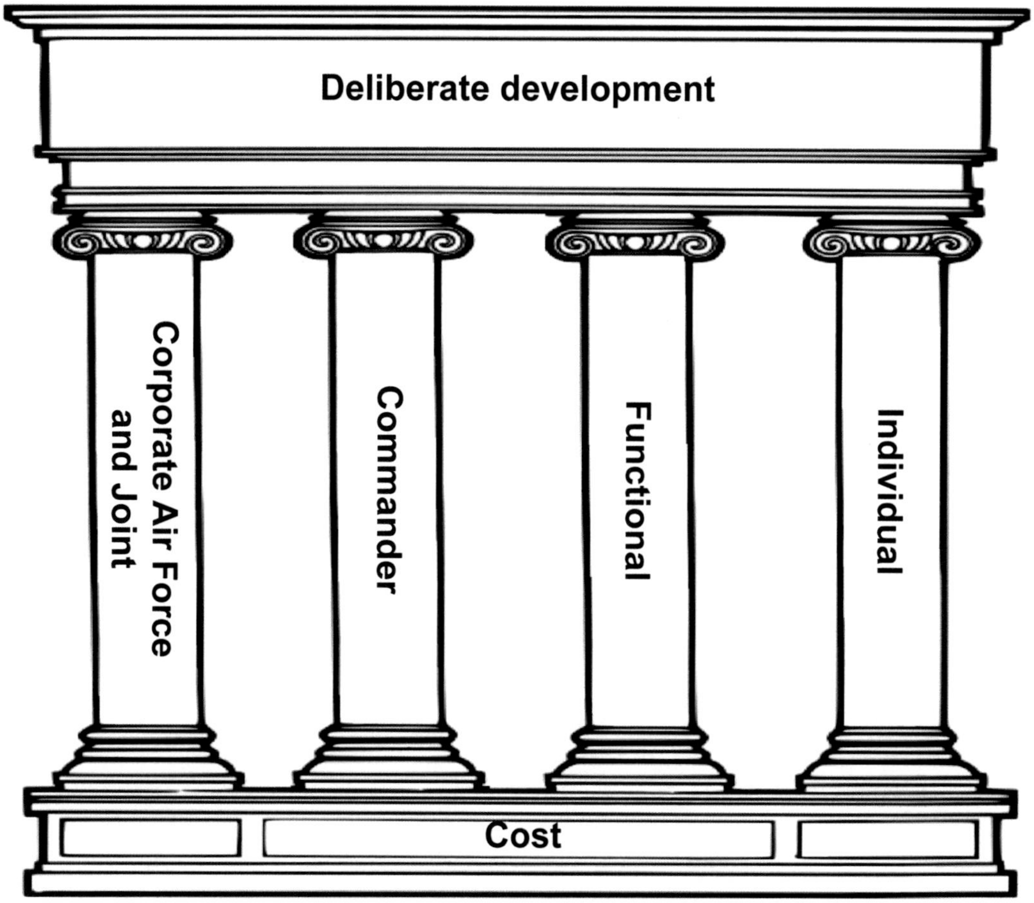

3

positions.[3] Commanders at wing level and above have a stake in having highly qualified officers to serve as squadron commanders. Commanders at all levels rotate through their positions relatively quickly, serving in any given command position for only a few years.

Thus, commanders' interests tend to focus more on meeting specific short-term needs for specific positions. Commanders do, however, also have functional (i.e., career field) medium- to long-term interests and are therefore interested in developing a sustainable pipeline of specialists for their career fields. Each career field has a functional interest in strengthening itself by ensuring a steady flow of qualified officers to meet staffing needs at increasing levels of responsibility. Finally, individual officers' interests are personal, focusing on how they can advance as career field specialists and Air Force officers.

The interests of each of these stakeholder groups must be provided for yet balanced against one another. Imbalanced relationships between stakeholder interests, especially in the long term, may hinder the effectiveness of developing the overall workforce. For example, there has been a perception among senior Air Force leaders that the current DT policies and practices disproportionately emphasize interests of the career fields in workforce development, with commanders' voices not being heard. If this perception is true, this imbalance would undermine the interests of the corporate Air Force, the Joint Staff, and commanders.

Purpose of the RAND Research

RAND was asked to examine the operations and effectiveness of the DTs and to recommend changes deemed important. Senior leaders had voiced two concerns about DTs. The first and loudest was that the influence of commanders on officers' careers had been diminished and that career field representatives (i.e., the functionals) had garnered too much influence.[4] The second was that, relative to the previous system of assignment teams, the DTs were too expensive.[5]

---

[3] This development goal is especially critical for military personnel in the Air Force, relative to nonmilitary personnel and organizations, because all senior military leaders must be developed from within the officer corps: There is no option to hire a senior military officer laterally if the development system has failed to create one. Failure to make a key development gate (e.g., in-residence PME, selection for command at one or more levels, or one or two below-the-zone promotions) can spell the difference between having a fully successful career that tops out at O-5 or O-6 and achieving general officer rank. DTs have to ensure that they are developing a sufficient cadre of high-potential officers in their functional or rated communities to fill senior leader requirements at O-6 and above.

[4] For example, before DTs began creating squadron commander candidate lists, individual MAJCOMs had administered the process, which placed the selection of squadron commanders squarely in the hands of MAJCOM commanders. DTs, which are functional area entities, are now in the middle of that process because they create command selection lists. MAJCOM commanders must choose subordinate commanders from the relevant lists DTs have prepared, even when they may desire to choose other specific individuals for command positions.

[5] As evidence of concern with the cost of DTs, AFPC (2012a) included an analysis of the cost of conducting DTs and began with a joint statement from the Secretary of the Air Force and the Chief of Staff: "We are committed to deliberate and ongoing process to enhance capabilities by reducing overhead and support functions and shifting resources to warfighter and readiness programs."

However, the essential charge to the RAND team was to conduct a comprehensive examination and review of DTs and their role in force development.

It soon became apparent that the Air Force was facing three essential options with regard to DTs: (1) Dismantle DTs altogether and return to a system of assignment teams; (2) continue forward with DTs as they currently operate; or (3) change some or all of the structure, functions, and operations of the DTs. Thus, the objective of this research was to examine the structure, functions, and operations of DTs in USAF force development and recommend which of the above three paths the Air Force should follow. This report summarizes the results of that study.

Methodology

We drew on qualitative and quantitative data in our examination of DTs. Table 1.1. lists the key data sources we used; references to specific materials are made throughout this report. To summarize, we reviewed historical documents to learn the original intention of senior leaders in approving the creation of DTs. We reviewed official Air Force policy documents and discussed policy with senior leaders, such as AF/A1 and AFPC/CC, and with DT chairs and AFPC staff. We observed three DT meetings: CAF, Contracting, and Logistics. Table 1.2 lays out the composition of these DTs and indicates the numbers of officers reviewed by the DT. We reviewed the minutes from the meetings of 19 different DTs. We reviewed a survey of DT experience and satisfaction that included responses from over 10,000 majors and lieutenant colonels (Near and Levin, 2011). We also reviewed how DTs had affected the development of individual officers' careers by working closely with AFPC and A1D staff, who produced critical

Table 1.1. Key Sources

Category	Specific Materials
Historical and background materials	Briefings to senior Air Force leaders describing proposed and planned changes to force development
Published Air Force doctrine on force development	AFIs, AFPDs
Annual instructions provided to DTs	A1 directives, PSDMs, AFPC briefings to DTs
DT-specific materials and interviews	DT charters, Developmental Education Designation Board (DEDB) briefing, DT minutes, stakeholder interviews
DT-specific materials and survey	U.S. Air Force DT 2011 Officer Experience and Satisfaction Survey (LMI, 2011)
Quantitative data	Official Air Force personnel files

Table 1.2. Development Team Meeting Data

DT	DT Composition	Majors in Career Field(s)	Lieutenant Colonels in Career Field(s)
Logistics	1 major general 12 colonels 1 lieutenant colonel, 1 civilian	341	245
Contracting	1 major general 8 colonels 2 civilians	136	119
CAF	1 major generals 2 brigadier generals 17 colonels	2,146	1,314

NOTE: Officer counts as of FY 2013.

results from official Air Force personnel data files.[6] The results of AFPC analyses drove individual and group discussions with key Air Force leaders, including AF/A1, AFPC/CC and AF/A1D. These discussions took place regularly throughout the conduct of this research.

Organization of This Report

Section 2 traces the original purpose of DTs in the force development system. Section 3 describes current DT policies and practices. Section 4 discusses recommended courses of action for the key functions of DTs.

---

[6] We shared the results of these analyses in closed meetings with AF/A1, AFPC/CC, and their senior staffs, but the sensitivity of the results of these analyses precludes including them in this public report. However, to illustrate the kinds of analyses we undertook and the level of their sensitivity, together with AFPC and A1D staff, we examined such questions as the following: Which officers were selected by DTs for in-residence PME, and what was their standing in promotion board scores? How did the officers selected by DTs who had attended in-residence PME fare in later promotions relative to officers who were in-residence "school selects" based on promotion board scores? Did it matter which in-residence PME an officer attended in terms of downstream promotions? Did timing of in-residence attendance at PME matter in terms of downstream promotions?

2. The Origin of Development Teams

During the September 2002 Corona, senior Air Force leaders were briefed on a new plan for force development (Hassan, 2002). At that time, it was argued that force development had focused only on the skills needed in each specific career field or stovepipe. Less attention was being paid to the enduring competencies that are required of all officers or to development that crossed career fields and prepared officers for future assignments outside their career fields that they might face at higher ranks and in later stages of their careers (see Figure 2.1).

Part of the reasoning behind this change was that senior leaders at or above the rank of colonel, such as wing commanders, commonly oversee officers and activities from outside of their career fields. For example, the commander of a flying wing will likely have operations, maintenance, mission support, and medical group commanders reporting to him or her who together are responsible for nearly the entire array of specialties and activities found in the Air Force. Although guided by officers in other specialties, a wing commander may be called on to make decisions directly affecting actions outside his or her primary specialty. Thus, more-senior

**Figure 2.1. Justification Provided to Corona in 2002 for a
New Force Development System**

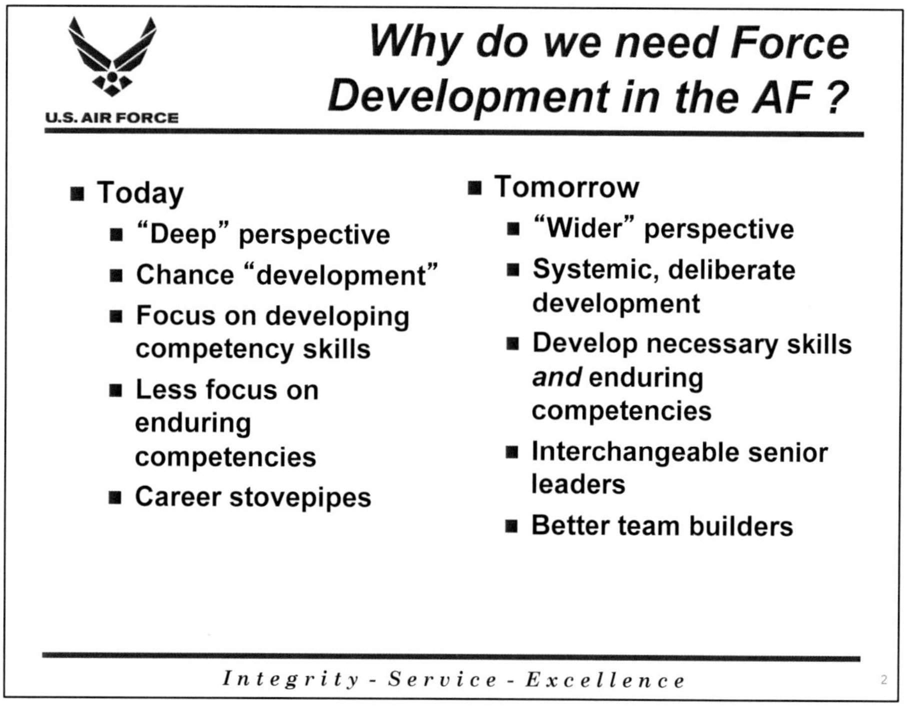

U.S. AIR FORCE

Why do we need Force Development in the AF ?

- Today
  - "Deep" perspective
  - Chance "development"
  - Focus on developing competency skills
  - Less focus on enduring competencies
  - Career stovepipes

- Tomorrow
  - "Wider" perspective
  - Systemic, deliberate development
  - Develop necessary skills *and* enduring competencies
  - Interchangeable senior leaders
  - Better team builders

Integrity - Service - Excellence

officers often find some level of familiarity or expertise outside their specific career fields to be valuable.[7]

In 2002, the Air Force leadership was seeking to improve how the Air Force personnel system prepared officers for the future. That improvement entailed creating a simple, understandable, deliberate development system for airmen that

- satisfied the skill needs of specific career fields and the need for enduring competencies
- had coordinated policies that focused on providing experience, education, and training at the right time in each officer's career
- best utilized the limited time for the PME components of force development
- balanced individual desires against Air Force needs.[8]

The force development concept proposed at that time differentiated occupation-specific skills that are required for successful performance in each career field from enduring competencies that contribute to successful performance regardless of career field or position (see Figure 2.2).

Figure 2.2. Necessary Skills and Notional Enduring Competencies

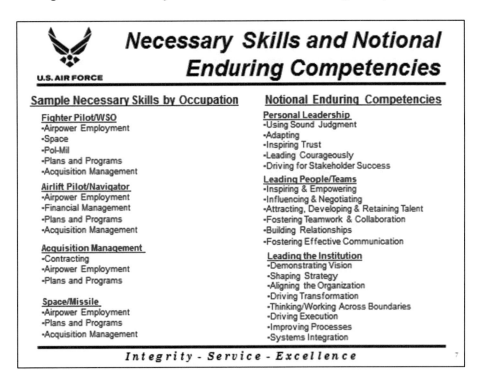

---

[7] Previous RAND research has supported the concept of what may be referred to as "skill pairing," which identifies the career fields that senior officers would find useful in addition to their primary career fields (for example, Robbert et al., 2004, and Moore, Thomas, and Conley, 2010).

[8] It is worthwhile to note that, only a few years earlier, in 1999, the Air Force did away with a voluntary assignment system and returned to a select-and-assign system. This change gave greater weight to the needs of the Air Force than had been the case under the previous, voluntary assignment system.

Furthermore, pairs of occupation-specific skills were identified as useful for officers progressing in specific career fields. For example, fighter pilots and weapon system officers could also be expected to need skills in airpower employment or acquisition management in later career assignments. Examples of enduring competencies included personal leadership (e.g., using sound judgment, inspiring trust), leading people and teams (e.g., inspiring and empowering; attracting, developing, and retaining talent), and leading the institution (e.g., demonstrating vision, improving processes). The primary objective of the newly proposed force development system was to manage the deliberate development of officers such that they would attain both the occupation-specific skills and the enduring competencies appropriate for each stage of their careers.

Officers pass through several levels of responsibility as they advance in their careers: tactical, operational, strategic, and senior leader (see Figure 2.3). Junior officers are focused on leading teams of people at a tactical level. For example, a fighter pilot at this stage of his or her career may advance as far as becoming a flight lead. The operational phase of a fighter pilot's career may include becoming a squadron commander or operations officer for a squadron. The strategic phase includes group or wing leadership positions. Finally, a senior leader's strategic role as a fighter pilot may include leading an air operations center, a numbered Air Force, or even a large aircraft or weapon system acquisition program. Similar career paths spanning tactical through senior leader phases can be identified for officers in other career fields.

Figure 2.3. Enduring Competencies, by Career Development Phase

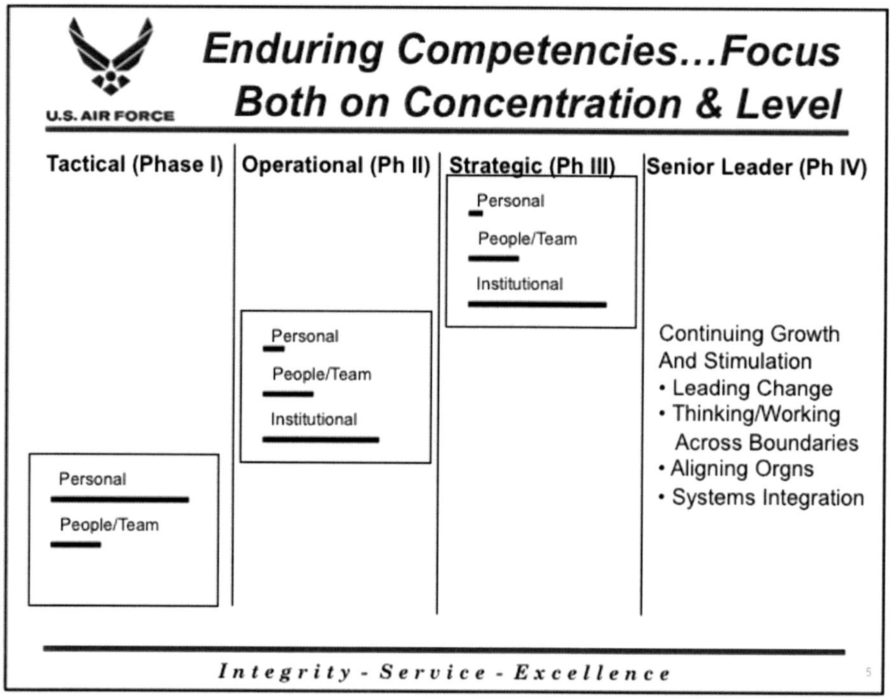

This vision for executing deliberate force development recognizes that PME and assignments together constitute the key elements of development and that these two elements go hand in hand throughout an officer's career. That is, each level of PME is designed to prepare officers for the challenges they will face prior to their next PME opportunity. Hence, the commissioning sources prepare college students and graduates to perform their duties on commissioning as lieutenants; Squadron Officer School prepares officers to perform as captains and majors; IDE, such as Air Command and Staff College, prepares officers to perform as lieutenant colonels; and SDE, such as Air War College, prepares officers to perform as senior lieutenant colonels and colonels. Seen in this light, two key Air Force organizations are responsible for development: The Air Education and Training Command is responsible for the formal education elements of force development, and AFPC controls assignments for officers below the grade of colonel. Together, these two organizations are charged with producing a synchronized and tailored development system aligned with the tenets of the then–newly proposed force development system to meet Air Force needs.

Operationalizing deliberate and systematic force development requires translating these broad goals into specific actions that support career fields, Air Force organizations, and individuals (see Figure 2.4). The Air Force's plan for operationalizing force development was intended to have two major components (U.S. Air Force, 2002; McMahan, 2002). First, an

Figure 2.4. Operational Plan for Creation of New Force Development System

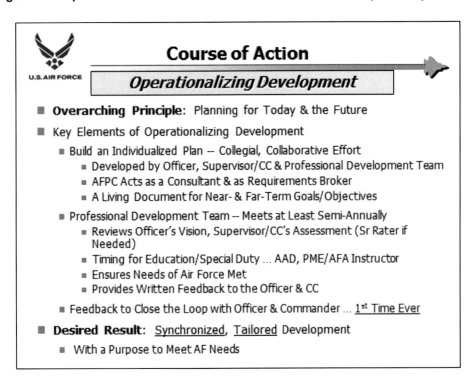

individualized development plan would serve as a modifiable, updatable, "living" document of near- and far-term goals and objectives. This plan would be built collaboratively by the officer, his or her supervisor or commander, and a professional development team (what is now known as the DT), with AFPC acting as a consult and requirements broker. The DT was the second key element of the proposal to operationalize development. The DT would meet semiannually to review officers' plans and performance assessments from supervisors and commanders (and sometimes senior raters). Finally, the DT would provide feedback to both the officer and his or her supervisor or commander. This feedback was intended to close the loop between the officer and his or her commander.

3. Current Development Team Practices

This chapter examines the current policies and practices of DTs.[9] To understand how DTs have evolved and how they balance often competing interests, we compared the purposes for which they were originally intended with how they have been implemented, including the degree to which DTs adhere to provided guidance. Our comparison began with a review of relevant policy documents. In addition, we conducted a series of discussions with Air Force senior leaders, policymakers, and DT chairs. This chapter summarizes highlights from these activities.

Air Force Policy Documents Direct and Guide Development Teams

Current policies and practices that we reviewed include

- AFIs that specify authoritative strategic guidance to DTs[10]
- Air Force Deputy Chief of Staff for Manpower, Personnel and Services (AF/A1) memos and directives that provide annually updated guidance to DTs
- AFPC briefings given at the DT meetings
- DT charters and recorded minutes of DT meetings.

Guidance Emphasizes Balancing Institutional, Functional, and Individual Needs

DT members typically include a general officer or equivalent civilian as chair, colonels representing MAJCOMs and wings, a career field manager, and an assignment team representative. For example, the July 2010 CAF DT was chaired by a brigadier general and included 22 colonels. The August 2011 Security Forces DT was chaired by a colonel and included 13 colonels. Most DT charters specify that membership is restricted to officers with a grade of O-6 or above. DTs review officer records and produce career guidance. DTs usually meet twice per year, often in person at AFPC, to discuss and determine vectors and recommended assignments for officers in their career fields. Inputs to this process include officer records. Outputs include command lists, selection of officers for DE (in addition to those already selected as part of a promotion board), vectors, and feedback. DT charters specify one to three

---

[9] DT practices and the vocabulary describing them in this document were current when the research was undertaken. For example, as of the date of this publication, *steady-state vectoring* is now referred to as *developmental vectoring*. Furthermore, the recommendations in this report were widely discussed with Air Force policymakers at the time, and some policies current at the time of this research were changed as a result of these recommendations.

[10] Although *strategic* and *tactical* have different meanings in different Air Force and military contexts in general, we use *strategic guidance* to refer to published AFIs, Air Force Policy Directives (AFPD), and similar official publications. We use *tactical guidance* to refer to letters, memos, briefings, and similar guidance from AF/A1 and AFPC provided to DTs just prior to or at their meetings.

meetings per year. In addition to broad strategic guidance that outlines DT roles and responsibilities, there is also strategic guidance for specific DT functions or particular subgroups.

Current strategic guidance for DT roles and responsibilities suggests that the Air Force intends for DTs to balance the interests of multiple stakeholder groups. This guidance is provided mainly in AFIs and AFPDs that deal with force development. In particular, AFI 36-2640 implements AFPD 36-26, *Total Force Development*. According to these documents, DTs manage force development for officers and civilian equivalents. AFI 36-2640 specifies that DTs must balance institutional and functional requirements and ensure that senior leaders understand that balance.

Placing DTs squarely in between force development systems and individual needs suggests that DT responsibilities are to fulfill both functional and corporate requirements (e.g., creating command lists) and to consider the needs and desires of individuals (translating force development policies into career vectors). These multifaceted roles and obligations require DTs to find a way to balance various needs and preferences. However, strategic guidance implicitly emphasizes functional, corporate, and mission requirements over meeting the needs and desires of individual officers or civilians. For example, the language in several AFIs directs DTs to implement officer and civilian personnel development such that it meets "both functional and Air Force corporate leadership requirements" (AFI 36-2640, p. 17) or "support(s) current and projected mission capabilities" (AFI 36-2640, p. 10).

Although the DTs do not control either assignments or promotions, their actions influence both. Assignment teams may take account of recommended vectors in the assignment process, and promotion boards have visibility of developmental assignments and in-residence school attendance. AFI 36-2110, *Assignments*, states that the Air Force supports individual airmen's educational goals, but not at the expense of "the overall best interest of the AF." AFI 36-2501, *Officer Promotions and Selective Continuation*, also suggests that the main objective of the promotion program is to further the objectives of the Air Force:

> The fundamental purpose of the officer promotion and federal recognition program is to select those officers best qualified to meet the needs of the Air Force. A promotion is not a reward for past service; it is an advancement to a higher grade based on future potential as demonstrated by past performance. (p. 63)

Individual qualifications are the stated primary criteria for assignments (AFI 36-2110) and general officer promotion (AFI 36-2501), implying that such factors as career field health are less relevant or secondary considerations.

AFI 36-2110 establishes criteria for assigning personnel in a way to satisfy multiple (i.e., operational, rotational, and training) requirements. The centralized assignment system seeks to ensure compliance with laws and directives and that assignments are effective and equitable. AFI 36-2501 establishes objectives for promoting officers to ensure that the best-qualified officers are promoted and to maintain "the necessary career incentive to attract and maintain a quality officer force" (p. 12).[11] Two specific criteria relate to interests of the overall Air Force—to "promote officers of the desired quality and quantity," and to "maintain strength in each grade for each competitive category (AFI 36-2501, p. 12). This AFI also outlines specific roles in the promotion process for commanders, senior raters, eligible officers, and central selection board (CSB) members and notes the need to maintain the officer corps' confidence in "the integrity of the selection process" (AFI 36-2501, p. 10).

Development Teams Also Receive Detailed Annual Guidance

Each year, AF/A1 issues a memorandum to functional managers and DT chairs that contains guidance for the DTs. This guidance typically restates the DTs' enduring goal of force development, referring to the policies (AFIs) and the overall strategic goal that DTs should focus on individual development of "fully-qualified mission ready Airmen" (Jones, 2012). It also directs DTs to perform various development functions and identifies specific priorities (force development special interest areas) for that year. For example, the memorandums from 2010 to 2012 advise developing broad skill sets across functional communities (e.g., the nuclear enterprise, irregular warfare, command and control operations) and providing tracking tools for inventory and requirements. Other guidance from the memorandums includes advising that functional advisory councils, if established, should be used for strategic discussions so that DTs can "focus more on the individual development of [their] Airmen during the DT." The memos also mention "close coordination between DTs and assignment teams," "key and critical billets," joint duty assignment list billets, and desirability of "mandated follow-on assignments" and "efforts to improve and standardize" DTs (Jones, 2011, as reproduced in Appendix B).

In addition to this annual AF/A1 memo, DTs receive other tactical guidance to help them fulfill strategic force development requirements, such as an AFPC briefing presented at DT meetings in 2012 DTs at AFPC (AFPC, 2012a). The purpose of the AFPC briefing is to ensure that DT members "understand Air Force developmental requirements" (slide 5, talking points). The briefing describes how a DT contributes to DE, provides vectors, and "shapes future state of leadership" (slide 7. It lays out a process in which DTs should use their knowledge of their career fields, including their career field's demographics, emerging needs and requirements, quality-of-force factors, and compliance with Air Force policies, to articulate the needs of the career fields. According to the briefing, the DTs then translate these career field needs into vectors for individual officers. The AFPC briefing also describes how AFPC operationalizes metrics of career field health and other performance measures, such as the percentage of officers whose next assignment matches their DT vector.

---

[11] AFI 36-2501 (p. 12) implies that such an incentive will exist if the promotion system is (1) "fair and equitable," (2) provides opportunities for "accelerated promotion" for exceptional officers, (3) maintains the appropriate number of officers in each grade and competitive category, and (4) provides "reasonably stable, consistent, and visible career opportunities."

Some of this tactical guidance focuses on managing DE. For example, one AFPC briefing (McKey, 2012) provided an overview of the DE process (e.g., composition of DEDB boards) and DTs' role in nominating individuals for DE programs. Also of note was its mention of improving joint performance (describing a need for DTs to help) to ensure that the Department of Defense requirement to maintain a joint tour length of 36 months is met, rather than needing to provide a waiver for individuals. Other tactical-level guidance regarding DE included AFPC, 2012b, which provided guidance and implementation instructions about IDE, SDE, and civilian developmental education (CDE). Its stated goal was to "integrate Senior Rater . . . and Development Team (DT) inputs with IDE/SDE/CDE opportunities and meet the developmental needs of the AF and its officers/civilians."

Official Policies Guide the Four Major Responsibilities of Development Teams

DTs have a number of responsibilities, among them these four specific tasks:[12]

- Provide general guidance to the assignment team regarding future assignments for each officer (steady-state vectoring) (AFI 36-2640, para. 3.5.4).
- Create a list of officers eligible to be selected for squadron command positions (AFI 36-2640, para. 3.5.12).
- Manage DE timing and school assignment for officers that a CSB has selected for in-residence schooling (school selects) and officers the DT has selected for in-residence schooling (candidates), (AFI 36-2640, para. 3.5.12).
- Provide feedback to officers (AFI 36-2640, para. 3.5.11).

Provide Steady-State Vectoring

AFI 36-2640 (p. 19) defines a vector as

> The DT's collective recommendation for an assignment level (e.g., Joint Staff, Air Staff, MAJCOM, base-level, etc.), training or education opportunity (e.g., resident DE, advanced functional training), or position type (e.g., flight commander, division chief, instructor, special duty, etc.) a member should be considered for in his or her next or subsequent assignments.

According to AFPC, 2013b, DTs should provide up to three vectors per individual. Annually updated guidance from AF/A1 directs DTs to vector best-qualified individuals to key assignments, identifies high-priority areas for education and assignments (e.g., Inspector General or language, region, and culture assignments), and provides some specific guidance (e.g., DTs should consider mandated follow-on assignments; DTs should work closely with assignment teams).

---

[12] See Appendix C. A 2010 briefing highlighted the first three tasks listed here (AFPC, 2012a).

DTs receive specific guidance on how to produce vectors. An example of an AFPC briefing to DT meetings (AFPC, 2012a) includes steady-state vectoring for programs and assignments as one of the DTs' major responsibilities, with some specifically mentioned as needing specific types of officers. Another AFPC briefing (McKey, 2012) states that DTs should translate their knowledge of the particular needs of their career fields into career vectors for individual officers, also factoring in commander recommendations, officer preferences and qualifications, leadership potential for IDE and SDE schools, and other considerations, such as follow-on assignments. This briefing also lists specific guidance on vectoring for IDE programs (i.e., when and where to vector individuals in their first or last years of eligibility, or "first-look" and "third- or last-look" designees, respectively), the Advanced Studies Group, and SDE programs and on policy for when to select or nominate for in-residence credit.

Most DT charters, as part of a standardized set of roles and responsibilities, mention that they will select individuals for special programs; maintain a career field prioritization plan and career field pyramid; and review officers' Airman Development Plans (ADPs), policies, and career guidance materials. These charters, however, do not offer much detail on how to provide vectors.

According to their published meeting minutes, the majority of DTs provide officers in their respective career fields with vectors at specified points in their careers. The point of the vectors is to provide officers and AFPC officer assignment teams with recommended future assignments designed to provide the officer with appropriate professional development, breadth, and knowledge in the Air Force. These vectors, however, can differ across DTs in timing or scope (i.e., generic vectors within the functional field, special-duty vectors). For example, some DTs allow senior rater–requested vectors, while other DTs vector officers who request it on their ADP.

Assignment officers get the vectors directly from the DTs. These officers facilitate the vectoring discussions during the DT meetings and input the vectors directly into the DT Tool (a software system designed to facilitate DT meetings) during the DT meetings. During the assignment process, assignment officers use the vectors to balance the Air Force mission needs against officer professional development.[13]

Create Command Lists

The overarching goal of promotions is to further the objectives of the Air Force, promoting officers who are best qualified to meet the needs of the Air Force. Individual qualifications are the stated primary criteria for assignments (AFI 36-2110) and general officer promotion (AFI 36-2501). Written guidance on command nominations states that DTs, as part of a centralized AFPC function, are responsible for selecting nominees in all eligible career fields, except space and missile operations (13S) and Mobility Air Force (AFPC, 2012a, slide 8). DT members are to base their selections on "commander recommendations, officer desires, background/goals/

---

[13] Personal communication from John Crown, AFPC/DSY, December 22, 2014.

aptitude, and potential to lead at higher levels within the field" (AFPC, 2012a, slide 8). Put another way, DTs are intended to recommend candidates in a manner that supports the Air Force practice of "commanders hire commanders" (AFPC, 2012a, slide 8).

Most DT charters state that DTs will select squadron commander candidates or participate in squadron commander selection boards and other special boards "as needed." Indeed, according to published DT meeting minutes, most DTs nominate candidates for command opportunities.

Manage Developmental Education

The Air Force has a limited number of in-residence school seats to fill. Officers are selected to attend in-residence IDE or SDE through two processes. First, the top 15 to 20 percent of officers, as scored by the O-4 and O-5 promotion boards, are guaranteed to attend in-residence schooling. These officers are referred to as *school selects*. Although they are guaranteed to attend, the timing and location depend on a number of factors both within and outside the control of the DTs. Second, DTs can select a limited number of officers who are being reviewed by the DT to attend in-residence schooling.[14]

Strategic guidance for force development states that DTs should manage education for the purpose of developing officers for the corporate and functional Air Force (e.g., AFPD 36-26, AFI 36-2640). Other strategic guidance states that the individual airman's educational goals should not supersede the overall best interest of the Air Force.

Annually provided guidance reminds the DTs of the importance of DE. Guidance from AF/A1 identifies high-priority areas for education and assignments (e.g., Inspector General or language, region, and culture assignments). AFPC briefings at annual DT meetings also outline the DTs' role in nominating individuals for DE programs (AFPC, 2012a; McKey, 2012). AFPC, 2012b, provides guidance and implementation instructions about IDE, SDE, and CDE. Stating that DTs are a "critical link to the nomination/designation function of the DEDB" (p. 1) it lays out the process DTs use to nominate officers and civilians in their career field to the Air Force DEDB or CDE Selection Board, respectively. Using these DT rankings and recommendations, DEDB matches nominees to available DE programs.

Most DT charters state an objective of deliberately developing leaders who will possess competencies and capabilities to meet Air Force missions and requirements. This objective is to be met by providing appropriate education, training, and experience. Most DT charters also list a standardized set of roles and responsibilities, including identifying developmental assignments and educational opportunities to match with candidates.

---

[14] Because the vagaries of having more than one promotion board to the rank of major or lieutenant colonel in some years result in larger numbers of school selects and because fewer in-residence school seats are available due to budget reductions, A1 has approved a method AFPC recommended to bring the numbers of officers selected by promotion boards to attend in-residence school and available seats back into balance. As a result, over the next several years, DTs will have very limited ability to send the officers not selected for in-residence schooling by the promotion boards to in-residence schooling.

Provide Feedback to Officers

Strategic-level guidance states that DTs should provide feedback to career field managers to update career field pyramids,[15] as well as "aggregate feedback" to officers and civilians, with senior raters to have primary responsibility for providing mentoring and feedback to individuals (AFI 36-2640). In particular, AFI 36-2640, para. 3.5.11 specifies that "DTs will provide career feedback to officers, civilians, senior raters, and commanders via the automated Airmen Development Plan system or other similar process" but does not specify what feedback content should be included.

DTs also receive more-detailed guidance on feedback annually; the emphasis is on giving personalized, concrete feedback. Guidance from AF/A1 directs DTs to provide general feedback in a couple of different ways: DT minutes, which should provide "actionable guidance" to airmen, and a webinar, which should be used to communicate results of DT meetings to the career field. AFPC guidance also describes procedures for disseminating feedback. For example, in a memo disseminated at a 2012 AFPC DT meeting, the AFPC commander directed the CAF DT to provide both general and tailored feedback to officers across the career field: "Upon completion of the DT, we are encouraging all DTs to 'broadcast' general feedback to their officers in the field via a live webinar in addition to personalized feedback via the system tool and publishing minutes" (Stewart, 2012).

The discussion of deliverables for which the DTs are responsible (AFPC, 2012a, slide 6), does not mention career feedback to individual officers.

What Do Development Teams Themselves Say They Do?

We also discussed policy with multiple stakeholders across the Air Force's force development system. These included representatives of A1D and AFPC and members of DTs. We invited all DT chairs for policy discussions regarding the tasks they performed, their views on the development process, and their suggestions for improvement. We also received input from individual Air Force officers regarding their personal experiences with the DTs.

Development Team Charters' Objectives, Purposes, and Goals

The DT charters describe the activities and goals each DT intends to pursue, serving as a point of comparison with guidance that was given to the DTs. Although strategic and annual or tactical guidance is provided generally to all DTs, there may be some natural variance across what DTs do, particularly given differences between individual career fields.

---

[15] Providing information to career field managers to update career field pyramids as needed is one of the DT responsibilities listed in AFI 36-2640, para. 3.5.1. Career field managers are permanent members of the relevant DTs and presumably obtain this information during DT meetings. However, we did not examine this DT responsibility during this research.

For the most part, DT charters are quite similar to each other. This is not surprising, as AFI 36-2640 provides a template for DT charters to follow. Indeed, most DT charters cite AFI 36-2640, and some charters also cite AFI 36-36 or the Chief of Staff of the Air Force (CSAF) Sight Picture.

As noted above, most DT charters state a general objective of deliberately developing leaders who will possess competencies and capabilities to meet Air Force missions and requirements. This objective is to be met by providing appropriate education, training, and experiences. A notable exception is the Cyberspace DT charter, which does not mention an objective but rather seems mostly focused on the process (e.g., DT's role as conduit between force development frameworks and individuals' needs). Another exception is the Financial Management DT charter, which lists no roles and responsibilities, perhaps because the charter we reviewed is relatively old, dating from February 21, 2006.

Examples of other activities mentioned in DT charters include maintaining a career field prioritization plan and career field pyramid; reviewing ADPs, policies, and career guidance materials; advising the functional community through career field managers; and others.

Discussions with Development Team Chairs

We discussed policy with DT chairs to learn more about the tasks they performed and their views on the development process, as well as to hear their suggestions for improvements. The interview protocol in Appendix A guided but did not limit these discussions.

We met with as many of the DT chairs as possible within a short time frame. We reached out to each of the 30 DT chairs but were unable to contact four of them. We heard back from and subsequently interviewed or received written input from DT chairs and staff from 11 of the 30 DTs. In some cases, multiple DTs shared the same chair, meaning that a single interview in fact reflected the experiences of several DTs.

The DT chairs who provided input had served in that role from 1.5 to 3 years. The membership of their DTs consisted of 16 to 20 officers, who generally were sitting commanders. The DTs held one to three meetings per year. DT chairs indicated that they were responsible for between 275 and 4,000 officers within their career fields. This wide variation in career field sizes is an important factor in their approaches to managing development.

Development Teams Prioritized Air Force and Career Field Goals but Differed on How to Achieve Them

In interviews, the DT chairs generally stated their objectives as developing leaders to fulfill career field needs and to achieve the Air Force mission but also broadening individuals by providing appropriate education and experiences. Some DTs simply stated that their objective was to support the overall Air Force mission. Others asserted that fulfilling the needs of the career field was necessary and the best way to achieve the Air Force mission. Still others acknowledged some conflict between functional and corporate needs (as well as those of the individual) and said that they attempted to find the proper balance. Most DT chairs (in both large and small career fields) explicitly mentioned that their goals were broad—that is, to manage and grow the entire force.

Although DT chairs typically stated generally similar objectives, they differed on a wide range of dimensions relating to how to achieve those goals. One divergence was in the scope of the DTs' focus and responsibilities. One DT chair from a small career field mentioned that the team focused narrowly on developing future general officers and senior leaders only, while a large DT focused only on developing majors and lieutenant colonels to meet more-immediate needs. Several larger career fields (i.e., those managing around 1,000 or more officers) and two small career fields developed multiple levels of leadership, with multiple DTs that each focused on different levels (e.g., one focuses on lieutenant colonels, one focuses on majors).

Several DT chairs described how they managed high-potential officers and revealed two fairly distinct approaches that did not appear to break down by career field size.[16] Two representatives of DTs for large career fields and one for a small career field stated that they did not actively manage high-potential officers but simply monitored their career trajectories. They provided high-potential officers with opportunities and allowed them to grow and develop, evaluating them along the way. One of the chairs of a large career field DT stated that, rather than focusing solely on high-potential officers, they wanted to set "realistic expectations for all O-4s and O-5s." This, they stated, was due to the need to "ensure each part of pyramid is appropriately sized. The goal is not just to grow future generals; developing colonels to fill senior roles is only part of DT process." In contrast, representatives of two DTs (one each for small and large career fields) actively manage their high-potential officers and assign them to important positions (e.g., large, complex squadrons). One of these DT chairs described this approach as part of their larger development strategy to "manage personnel through the right leadership billets to accomplish the mission and further develop officers."

Comments from Development Team Chairs and Members on Their Major Responsibilities

We interviewed or received written responses to our questions from the chairs of the a number of DTs (listed here) on how the DTs conduct activities in the four major responsibilities described earlier in the chapter, along with several other miscellaneous functions:

- Airfield Operations
- Ammo, Munitions, and Logistics Readiness
- Biomedical Science Corps (written comments)
- Chaplain
- CAF

---

[16] By general consensus, the DTs defined high-potential officers as those promoted below the zone to O-5.

- Contracting
- Dental
- Finance
- Special Operations (written comments)
- Special Investigations
- Weather.

The interviews began with the questions listed in Appendix A, but the subsequent discussions were open and ranged widely.

Provide Steady-State Vectoring

Interviews with DT chairs and officers suggested that the specificity and value of these vectors varied by career field. For example, one DT chair described vectoring in his career field as a "broad brush." In contrast, another career field held separate DTs for first-time majors and lieutenant colonels (IDE/SDE DT) and for officers newly graduated from first-time command (Command DT), issuing separate steady-state vectors for each. Another DT provided vectors by reviewing several Officer Performance Reports and Single Unit Retrieval Formats for each individual. The DT chair said that this was made possible by virtue of having a small career field, where "everyone knows everyone," presumably making it easier to tailor vectors to be more useful to individuals.

Vectors were often seen to provide little value. In a 2011 survey of officers by Near and Levin (2011), only 29 percent of majors and 37 percent of lieutenant colonels strongly agreed or agreed that the DT vectoring process is fair and equitable. Twenty-six percent of majors and 19 percent of lieutenant colonels in the same survey said they did not know where to find their DT vectors. Only about 50 percent of majors and lieutenant colonels who responded to the survey strongly agreed, agreed, or somewhat agreed that DT vectors helped them to achieve either short- or long-term career goals. One comment among the survey responses asking what is the DT program's greatest weakness was that "DT vectors are vague, with no direction and no explanation."

Create Command Lists

DT chairs stated that their DTs create command lists either for AFPC to pick from or for "commanders to hire commanders," often down to the squadron or flight level. These recommendations are based on their knowledge of individuals and squadron or flight needs. To allow flexibility, DTs may generate more names than positions (e.g., two to five names per position), then rank the individuals on the list to be sent to commanders. Some DTs then negotiate and deconflict commanders' picks, as needed. One DT mentioned that there is often a "pecking order," in which certain squadrons may hold greater influence, but there is generally no formal prioritization. The process is also personality dependent and can be influenced by strong commanders or the existence of personal relationships between DT members and individual officers.

Several DT chairs agreed that the responsibility for picking commanders was properly situated with DTs. One DT chair stated that a "core competency of the DT is picking commanders." Exercising command list flexibility was seen as a particular strength of DTs. As one DT chair pointed out, low density in a small career field will often mean that there are not enough people to send to squadrons, so "almost anybody will make it on the list." A commander's request for an alternate can ripple through the rest of the assignments, which the DTs can help manage. Another DT mentioned that the rationale for commanders' initial selection is that senior colonels serving on the DT know the complexity and size of their squadrons.

A comment Near and Levin (2011, slide 31) highlighted from their survey with regard to DTs and command lists was "In theory it gives senior leaders the ability to guide the midlevel leaders and ensure quality leaders are chosen for command positions. But reality is something different."

Manage Developmental Education

In selecting officers for DE opportunities, DTs intend to ensure that each officer receives appropriate training, jobs, or experience. To determine what opportunities are most appropriate, one DT chair, for example, based decisions on the required experience for higher pay grades (e.g., which types of experience majors would need to succeed as lieutenant colonels). One DT chair stated a preference for having a CSB perform IDE/SDE selection, which they thought would otherwise be unduly influenced by functional interests. Another DT chair mentioned identifying both the needs of the career fields and the capabilities required of people by grade in managing DE. This may be especially true of smaller career fields or of those with unique requirements. For example, as of the end of FY 2014, only 64 majors and 26 lieutenant colonels in the Air Force were specializing in airfield operations, compared to over 500 lieutenant colonels who were fighter pilots. Also, some line Air Force career fields, such as contracting, and nonline career fields, such as those in medical, dental, and legal, have unique DE requirements to support their technical skills. But these officers also fill leadership positions within their areas of expertise, so some also stand in need of DE opportunities, such as the Air Command and Staff College (ACSC) and Air War College (AWC).

Describing the results of DT efforts, one chair stated that officers in their career field attended mostly traditional IDE/SDE—specifically, most officers attend AWC; some attend Army War College or Navy War College; and a very few attend DE in France, Japan, Australia, or other locations. This DT chair also noted that his team had been "relatively successful" at placing officers from their alternate list into schools.

Provide Feedback to Officers

Feedback to officers varied widely, with some DTs emailing individuals directly or providing broader feedback through webinars or in the DT minutes. (Even the details of these minutes vary—some contain only high-level comments, while others contain detailed notes; furthermore, not all minute meetings were posted to the "MyDP" website.[17])

Several DT chairs suggested that they expected individual feedback to officers to come primarily from their commanders or chains of command. There was therefore some discussion of mentoring and its role in the feedback process. That is, the chairs suggested that providing individualized feedback from the DT could fall into the realm of mentoring or that mentoring provides a conduit for direct feedback. One DT chair mentioned that captains through lieutenant colonels in the career field were assigned mentors. Another DT chair, from a small career field, stated that their colonels had access to a direct mentoring process in which each was assigned a mentor (mostly picked by the colonels themselves). However, the results of mentoring has been viewed as "a mixed bag" because people move around and presumably are not able to devote much time to the mentoring relationship.

Views from the field appear to support the DT chairs' observations that individualized feedback is uncommon. Near and Levin (2011, slide 3) reported that "70% of respondents feel that their DTs do not communicate directly with them." They also reported that a common weakness respondents listed was "lack of direct feedback" (slide 4). Fifty percent of majors and 47 percent of lieutenant colonels disagreed or strongly disagreed with the statement, "My leadership discusses the DT process with me"(slide 20). Seventy-two percent of majors and 67 percent of lieutenant colonels disagreed or strongly disagreed with the statement, "My DT communicates directly with me" (slide 8).

Overall, feedback to individual officers appears inconsistent. Some DTs email members directly. Some DTs hold webinars. Some DTs provide feedback in the minutes. The level of detail in the minutes also differs: Some minutes contain only high-level comments or actions, while others contain detailed notes. Finally, not all minutes were made available.

Interviews with several Air Force officers also suggested that how career feedback is provided varies by the individual initiative of each career field but often comes with the assumption or expectation that the officer is aiming for top leadership positions (i.e., not for alternative career paths).

---

[17] From an interview with then Director of Force Development, Daniel Sitterly:

> My Development Plan [MyDP] is all about total force and is geared to help users make informed decisions about their career with information available at one site. MyDP's primary goal is to be the one stop shop for all career-related applications, from career progression to potential job assignments. MyDP already gives individuals instant access to their records, career field information and a consolidated career summary—all from one website. MyDP allows airmen to take a more proactive role in their career development by offering a web-based resource for education-, training-, and experience-related information and opportunities. (Sitterly, 2011)

As part of the United States Air Force Development Teams 2011 Officer Experience and Satisfaction Survey,[18] conducted by LMI (Near and Levin, 2011), Air Force officers answered several questions related to their experiences with feedback from the DTs. In addition, respondents were asked to write in open-ended comments. Many respondents took advantage of the opportunity to describe their personal experiences with DTs and suggested improvements. Much of this written commentary contained information related to feedback.

The authors reported several major feedback-related conclusions from the survey:

- Close to half (42 percent) of all respondents feel that DTs do not help them plan their career paths.
- Nearly half of the respondents are unaware of what information their DT reviews when it meets (39 percent), of when their DT meets (41 percent), and over half (52 percent), are unaware of the personnel that comprise their DT.
- 70 percent of respondents feel that their DTs do not communicate directly with them (Near and Levin, 2011, slide 3).

In addition, only 22 percent of respondents agreed that "the DT process is transparent" (Near and Levin, slide 8). Even though 83 percent of respondents knew where to find MyODP (the version of MyDP for officers), only 42 percent of respondents said that they used it for career planning.

Out of a total of 27,509 written comments, there were a number of common themes. Positive perceptions of DTs mostly related to their general intent: "Many respondents like the idea of the DT and the direct guidance they could receive on their career paths. Respondents believe in the concept and potential of the DT, but many say that there is a disconnect between the theory and the practical application of the program" (Near and Levin, slide 31). Negative perceptions of DTs related to operationalization, including lack of communication and transparency: "Common weaknesses listed by respondents included lack of communication between members and DT personnel, lack of direct feedback, lack of interaction, and a general lack of information surrounding DTs" (Near and Levin, slide 4). In response to questions about how DTs could be improved, respondents suggested "more feedback between members and DT personnel, timely feedback, better communication, and more transparency throughout the DT process" (Near and Levin, slide 4).

Based on these findings, the authors concluded that the DTs' "greatest weakness is communication with officers" (Near and Levin, slide 35). One specific recommended area of improvement to focus on was "immediate, detailed, and direct feedback to officers following DT vectors" (Near and Levin, slide 35). In particular, the authors suggested focusing on captains and majors, who are less aware of DT process and have had less communication with the DTs.

---

[18] Near and Levin (2011) reported that, at the time of the survey, the total survey population was 31,428 (presumably Air Force officers). The total number of survey responses was 12,927 (a response rate of 41 percent), of whom there were 2,722 captains, 5,588 majors, and 4,617 lieutenant colonels. The survey was fielded from September through October 2011.

In addition to these overall conclusions from the survey questions, we reviewed a small selection of the written comments for feedback-related content. A recurring theme was a lack of knowledge about DTs and how their feedback related to individuals' career goals and the broader needs of the Air Force. In particular, respondents described a lack of information from DT feedback about the needs of the Air Force and how they could plan their professional goals accordingly. There were also several mentions of lack of knowledge about how DTs operate, such as their membership and processes. In fact, some respondents stated that they were completely unaware of the DTs and what they do, for example: "I'm a lieutenant colonel with 27 years of service. I've never even heard of a development team. Think that might be a problem?"[19]

Lack of personalized feedback was another common theme. Multiple comments called for more feedback, specifically regarding vectors (e.g., more detailed guidance, details on how they had been determined). For example, one suggestion was to "publicize the intent of the vector." Respondents felt that vectors were too general to be of value and that mentorship was lacking. Several mentioned that DT feedback was late or not supplied when it would have been most useful. As an example of a vector that was not useful, one respondent mentioned receiving a vector that suggested, as a next career step, trying for the exact job that officer was currently assigned to. Respondents indicated that personalized feedback depended in large part on individual relationships, such as whether one's immediate supervisor was particularly helpful. Other officers pointed to the advantages of knowing members of the DT: "Time with the DT member was invaluable and extremely educational in helping me better fill out my ODP [officer development plan] and plan my long-term goals. Wish more people had that opportunity, especially those at lower ranks."

Respondents also suggested addressing perceptions of subjective feedback, including a lack of transparency about criteria for recommendations, potential biases based on "who you know." One officer noted, "Subjective rather than qualitative criteria for evaluation seems to result in DT members favoring the officers they know and have worked with, or at least creates the appearance of that." DTs were even compared to puppet masters and a secret society. As an example, one solution for remedying these perceptions was having DTs add contact information to recommendations so that individuals could follow up with questions.

Finally, respondents suggested a need for acknowledging the existence and value of alternate career paths, "that not everybody is trying to be the next CSAF." In the views of some respondents, a single-minded focus on a specific type of career path may lead to the perception that DTs write off officers who are no longer promotable: "Passed over shouldn't equate to forgotten. . . . There is no substitute for experience."

---

[19] The remaining quotations in this section, "Provide Feedback to Officers," are taken from open-ended comments made by respondents in the survey conducted by Near and Levin (2011).

Other Development Team Functions

Metrics

The DT chairs kept a variety of metrics on either individuals or the career field as a whole. Individual-focused metrics included the percentage of officers who receive an assignment consistent with their vectors. Career field–focused metrics included the percentage of quota filled for nominated positions. Some metrics, such as promotion rates, can serve as metrics for both individuals and career fields. Other examples of metrics included the diversity of members nominated or selected, overall retention and satisfaction within a career field, success of command tours, and trends in officers with command positions outside the career field. Finally, several DTs used no metrics or asserted that metrics should not necessarily be used to judge DT effectiveness. Instead, they asked themselves whether they were "spreading opportunities equally."[20]

Most DTs also monitor career field health and demographics through briefings from AFPC personnel. The DTs identify career field–specific issues (e.g., low field grade officer manning levels, outside core requirements, deployment rates). They also compare assigned with authorized numbers across, for example, manning, utilization, inventory, or sustainment versus attrition.

Process

DTs also took steps to prepare for future DT activities. These steps included ensuring the continuity of DT membership by prepping incoming members (e.g., verbal advice, shadowing current DT members) and building an audit trail for future DT chairs (e.g., keeping a list of output analyses).

General Recommendations for Change from the Development Teams

Most DT chairs expressed highly positive views of DTs, deeming them crucial or critical. They made statements such as, "We need [the DTs]," and "I consider DTs absolutely vital to mission success." Some DTs pointed out that, if there were no DTs, the functions would still have to be performed. One DT chair further noted that DTs provide transparency that improves perceptions among the force about the career development process.[21] DTs from both large and small career fields mentioned the opportunity to review and consider individual officers as one of the DTs' particular advantages, although they appeared to differ on how feasible this was. A DT chair from a large career field stated that the "biggest strength" of the DTs was an Air Force Specialty Code–wide view of officers, which "offered opportunity to identify officers not well

---

[20] Comment from our interviews with DT chairs.

[21] However, in a 2011 survey of officer experiences with and perceptions of DTs (Near and Levin, 2011), respondents indicated a strong lack of perceived transparency in the DT process. See the Section 4 for more details.

known." However, several DT chairs from smaller career fields stated that they were able to properly consider individual officers in their career fields only because their fields were small.

DTs generally agreed on how often DT meetings were needed and how they should be held. They did suggest that it would be acceptable to hold fewer DT meetings and that these could be held in conjunction with other existing meetings, rather than at AFPC (e.g., for one career field at their an annual leadership conference). DT chairs generally believed that face-to-face meetings were essential for the informal discussion ("the music is between the notes," one DT chair said), but virtual tools could supplement them. DTs differed on the preferred composition of DT membership, with some advocating for high-potential officers and others for commanders.

DTs also differed on whether standardizing DT processes across functional areas was desirable or even possible. Currently, although they perform similar activities for providing officer development, training, and experiences, DTs do not appear to follow a standardized process. This may be because DT guidance is at times ambiguous about rules and operations, such as how to develop and structure career vectors and feedback, and even membership requirements. For example, AFI 36-2640 states that membership is "ideally" composed of general officers or senior executive service personnel, and that the Air Reserve Component is "highly encouraged" to establish and use DTs. This provides leeway and perhaps confusion when situations are not "ideal," allowing DTs to determine for themselves what to do. Although several DT chairs suggested that some standardization was desirable, those from both small and large career fields expressed doubt. A DT chair stated that greater standardization would hurt smaller career fields that might have just one or two qualified individuals for a given position. Another DT chair stated that large career fields (e.g., CAF) might not have the capacity to pick and choose individuals to recommend for DE or command, particularly because they had many options to choose from.

Do Development Teams Accomplish Their Four Primary Tasks?

Our a review of published DT meeting minutes and interviews with and comments from the chairs of several DTs indicate that the DTs focus most of their energy on accomplishing two of their tasks: (1) creating squadron command lists and (2) managing DE. As we note in the next chapter, there is room for improvement in how DTs perform these tasks.

We found that providing career vectors for the officers being reviewed was quite uneven across DTs. The unevenness is a function of two things. First, the DT role in assignment processes is generally limited to broad career vectors, such as recommending that an officer's next assignment be to a position in Air Force headquarters at the Pentagon, a position within the headquarters of a MAJCOM, or to a joint assignment. Second, depending on the career field or career fields the DT is responsible for, there may be a relatively large or small number of officers to receive vectors. For example, the CAF and Mobility Air Forces DTs review a large number of officers, while the Contracting DT reviews a smaller number of officers.

The fourth task of DTs is to provide feedback to officers. Feedback is provided via DT meeting minutes and a webinar, as indicated Jones, 2011 (see Appendix B). While it is fair to say that all DTs provide feedback, the level and value of the feedback are quite varied.

To summarize, the DTs accomplish their four tasks but do so with varied levels of success in terms of effectiveness, particularly in providing vectors and feedback. There are many opportunities for improvement in the performance of each of the DT tasks, which are highlighted in the next chapter.

4. Observations and Recommendations

Our review of the original intentions of Air Force leaders when they created the DTs suggests these leaders wanted to move away from "chance" development toward deliberate development that offers synchronized and tailored career development opportunities for individual officers but also wanted to balance functional and career field needs against corporate and officership needs. They considered DTs to be a critical part of the force development system. The official documents make it clear that Air Force leaders require DTs to perform four primary functions: (1) provide general guidance to the assignment team regarding future assignments for each officer ("steady-state vectoring"), (2) create a list of officers eligible to be selected for squadron command positions, (3) manage DE timing and school assignment for officers selected for in-residence schooling by a CSB ("school selects") and officers selected for in-residence schooling by the DT ("candidates"), and (4) provide feedback to officers. DT actions can either support or unintentionally undermine the interests of stakeholder groups, depending on the actions they take. Consider the following: The corporate Air Force has an interest in ensuring that senior-level positions (O-6 and higher) are filled by highly qualified officers and that Air Force officers compete successfully for important senior-level joint jobs; the Air Force and joint community also need qualified Air Force officers to represent an airpower perspective within joint organizations. While not impossible, it is difficult for so-called late bloomers to catch up with their year-group peers who have consistently been high-achieving officers. If a DT uses an in-residence PME seat for a late bloomer who is not likely to advance beyond O-5, it may deprive another officer, who does have the potential to advance further, of the opportunity to pass an important gate and perhaps rise to O-6 or higher. This thins the bench of officers who do have the potential to achieve ranks of O-6 and above. It takes a consistent career-long level of high achievement to reach the ranks of general officer, and late bloomers simply do not have that consistent career-long record of high achievement.[22]

---

[22] AFPC provided the specific data to support this statement in closed-door conversations among senior Air Force leaders, but the data are not available for presentation in a public forum because of their sensitivity. However, there is also a logical argument that supports this statement. Officer promotion boards review cumulative records in their decisionmaking, and competition for promotion to the ranks of colonel and above is fierce. Furthermore, all line officers compete against one another in promotions, regardless of career field. Officers with a steady record of below-the-zone promotion and attendance at in-residence DE are simply more competitive than those without a consistent record. For example, a top board score for promotion to major guarantees an in-residence seat for IDE. These two events, in turn, set that officer up for a potentially early promotion to lieutenant colonel. A top board score for promotion to lieutenant colonel then guarantees an in-residence seat for SDE. This kind of consistent record makes such an officer more competitive for promotion to colonel than an officer who has only one in-residence DE attendance on his or her record. On the other hand, an officer who does not attend IDE in residence is less likely to be promoted early to lieutenant colonel and therefore less likely to garner a guaranteed in-residence SDE seat. If a DT does give such an officer an in-residence seat to SDE, as a late bloomer, that officer will still be

As another example, consider the creation of command lists and how DTs can support commanders while balancing their own functions' needs to develop senior leaders. From a functional perspective, DT members, particularly in small functional areas, have a good understanding of which individual officers could most benefit from specific command experiences and which command assignments would most benefit the functional area. However, stacking the command list deck to ensure that specific individuals get specific commands serves the functional area at the expense of commanders' prerogatives to select commanders.

We reviewed and observed current policies and practices of DTs and reviewed the results of a survey on officer experience and satisfaction with DTs (Near & Levin, 2011). We found that, by and large, DTs prioritize Air Force and career field goals but differ on how to achieve them. These differences have varying impact on officers, especially high-potential officers. While DT chairs believe that their services add value to the force development system, they recommended changes to policies and practices. In this chapter, we summarize our observations, describe the conceptual framework we used, and provide recommendations.

Three Possible Courses of Action for the Future of Development Teams

We considered three broad options regarding DTs: continuing with the status quo, eliminating the DTs, and reforming them.

The first option we considered would be to leave the DTs in place as currently constructed, with the DTs retaining their roles and responsibilities and continuing to act as they do now. We found that leaving DTs as they are overvalues functional interests because DTs have come to focus on the health of their career fields. This current outcome is understandable because each DT naturally attempts to optimize outcomes for its own career field. However, for the corporate Air Force, DTs have a somewhat negative effect on the career progression of corporately identified high-potential officers when DTs thin the high-potential bench by advancing late bloomers for command and in-residence PME. Some DTs reduce the ability of commanders to hire commanders of their choosing. For individual officers, while DTs pay more attention to individual development, they do not all provide systematic feedback to individuals.

The second option is to eliminate the DTs. In this case, AFPC and career field managers would assume the responsibilities. Rather than deliberate career development managed by DTs explicitly charged with this responsibility, officer development would be left to the actions of individuals, assignment teams, functional managers, and commanders. However, this approach raises several unanswered questions that suggest that eliminating DTs would not yield better results. For the corporate Air Force, who would be responsible for strategic development—that is, creating a strong and deep bench of future Air Force leaders—the primary purpose for which DTs were created? Would commanders have fewer well-developed people to choose from? In

---

less competitive for promotion to colonel than the officer in the previous example. This is what we mean by thinning the bench because it results in fewer officers from a career field being competitive for promotion to colonel.

the functional community (i.e., career fields), would assignment teams and career field pyramids, combined with ad hoc mentoring, suffice to maintain strong career field senior leaders? Finally, would career development of individual officers also be left to ad hoc mentorship and one-off initiatives in response to changing signals from the Air Force? In short, if the DTs were simply eliminated, the force development system would revert to the personnel system prior to 2002. Therefore, the Air Force would be left with the shortcomings that were associated with that personnel development system.

The final option would be to reform the DTs by creating a better approach to deliberate development. This would entail standardizing DT processes, with the simultaneous aims of articulating corporate interests, increasing commanders' voice, sharpening functional influence, and providing better feedback to individuals.

Reforming the Development Teams

Our analysis of each course of action suggests we recommend the third option: reform the DTs. Our recommendation is based on two premises. The first is that DTs should be retained because deliberate development remains a worthy goal. The second is that DTs need to be reformed to bring the interests of all four stakeholders into balance.

DTs influence different elements of workforce development through their four major responsibilities. The following subsections discuss our observations on and recommendations for each of these and discuss strategic objectives.

Providing Steady-State Vectoring

Interviews with DT chairs and officers suggested that the value of steady-state vectors varied by career field, and the earlier survey (Near and Levin, 2011) confirmed that few officers use or see value in vectors, but perhaps this is the result of uneven or poor implementation. However, AFPC reports that assignment officers are on hand during DT meetings to aid in the discussion of vectors, record them in the DT Tool, and then refer them in the assignment process. The comments from DT chairs and the results of the LMI survey suggest that vectoring is not well understood or communicated. There is an emerging consensus to eliminate this as a required task for DTs. We concur with this emerging consensus in the context of requiring it for all officers being reviewed. However, some DTs reported actively managing their high-potential officers, and we recommend this as a strategic objective for all DTs:

> **Recommendation 1: DTs should no longer be required to provide steady-state vectors for all officers under review, but should continue to vector and begin to track the progress of high-potential officers.**

Managing Developmental Education

How DTs manage DE may be the most challenging issue in improving force development. Managing DE involves complicated decisionmaking about who will attend in-residence schools, where each officer will attend, and when they will attend. DT policies and guidance on this issue must therefore be crafted to ensure a balance among what is best for individual officers, what is best for the career field, and what serves the needs of the corporate Air Force.

The decisions DTs make play a role in determining who receives DE, where they go, and when they go. The challenge is to preserve the value that DTs add while minimizing undesirable second- and third-order effects.

Allocating In-Residence Class Seats to DTs

AFPC practice has been to allocate in-residence seats for candidates to DTs based on the size of the career field each represents. However, not all career fields have requirements for O-5 and O-6 officers that are related to the overall size of the career field. We believe this practice of sharing seats based on career field size should be changed to recognize that DE exists to prepare officers for positions they will hold at higher ranks. As a result, we recommend allocating in-residence seats to support each career field's needs for O-5 and O-6 officers:

> **Recommendation 2: School seats should be allocated to DTs to meet requirements for the number of lieutenant colonels and colonels needed to fill positions in each career field.**

This recommendation has several implications:

- Requirements for lieutenant colonels and colonels in operational and support career fields, rather than sheer field size, should drive the allocation of seats to DTs.
- AFPC should base IDE career field requirements for in-residence seats on each career field's requirements for lieutenant colonels.
- DPO should base SDE career field requirements for in-residence seats on each career field's requirements for colonels.
- Allocations across career fields should be smoothed over time to avoid large fluctuations in the pipeline of in-residence schooled officers in each career field.
- To smooth out the gaps that may result from allocation of too many or too few in-residence seats to CSB school selects, 20 percent of all seats should be reserved for DT candidates.[23]

Choosing Who Will Attend Developmental Education In-Residence

In an unpublished study undertaken by AFPC for the AF/A1 at the time, officers were categorized into three tiers. For a given CSB outcome, Tier 1 included the top 20 percent of

---

[23] These recommendations were presented to the Air Force while this research was in progress. Modifications were made to Air Force policies and this recommendation to smooth the demand for and allocation of in-residence seats was implemented.

officers; Tier 2 included the next 30 percent; and Tier 3 included those in the bottom 50 percent. As noted above, the Tier 1 officers are guaranteed in-residence attendance.

If the CSBs made all selections for in-residence DE, presumably reflecting corporate Air Force values, officers from Tier 2 would fill the in-residence seats the Tier 1 officers have not taken. All else equal, one might reasonably expect that the majority of candidates DTs select for in-residence schooling would come from Tier 2. However, AFPC analyses show that this is not the case. DT-selected candidates mostly came from Tier 3. Part of the reason for this may be that DTs select some officers for in-residence DE whom they refer to as "late bloomers." Presumably, these late bloomers might not have looked as qualified at the time of the CSB as they did by the time the DT reviewed them. Such choices may also result from DTs being able to share and discuss detailed and personal information about officers that was not available to the CSB—information provided to CSBs and open to discussion is strictly controlled, while DTs have and exercise much freer rein over what they can share and discuss. A final point in this regard is that DTs do not know the CSB scores and do not know which officers are in Tiers 2 and Tier 3. That is, they are not knowingly selecting Tier 3 officers over Tier 2 officers.

Nonetheless, the selection of Tier 3 officers over Tier 2 officers reduces the overall quality of the officer promotion pool moving forward. This tends to "thin the bench" because Tier 3 officers are unlikely to have had a history of consistent high-level performance, which is likely why the promotion board placed them in the bottom 50 percent. As a result, these individuals are less likely to become competitive colonels or general officers when rated by future promotion boards. In addition, the Tier 2 officers who may have been consistently high performers up to that point are effectively knocked out of the running to become competitive colonels or general officers because they did not get an in-residence school seat that was given to a Tier 3 officer instead.[24] This leads us to our next recommendation:

Recommendation 3: The Air Force should implement several changes to the selection of officers for in-residence DE.

In implementing this recommendation,

- The first principle should be that all CSB school selects go to in-residence programs. However, the number of CSB school selects should be capped at the top 20 percent of promotions, subject to future board schedules.[25]

---

[24] This point has become moot to some degree since 2013 because CSB school select officers are taking almost all in-residence seats. This has resulted from what might be considered a perfect storm: Large groups of officers meeting promotion boards, the guarantee that the top 15 to 20 percent will train in residence, and downward budgetary pressure on the number of in-residence seats available have left little room for DTs to send officers not selected for in-residence schooling by promotion boards to in-residence schooling.

[25] For example, fixing the number of CSB officers selected for in-residence schooling at 20 percent of promotions might swamp the available in-residence seats if the schedules mean the boards meet every two years instead of every year.

- DTs should continue to pick candidates when in-residence seats are available.[26]
- Some DT candidates should also go to in-residence programs. As with the CSB, the DT share of seats should be capped at 20 percent, subject to the availability of seats and other requirements.
- Nominations and "dream sheets" should be limited to officers who are eligible for promotion.
- Senior rater nominations should be capped at 10 percent of eligible candidates.
- AFPC Directorate of Assignments should annually sort officers for feasibility to go to school.[27]
- Implement "gray-zone" resolution system for identifying school selects at the CSB.[28]

Determining Where Officers Will Attend

Officers can attend many different in-residence programs for DE credit. Many of these programs have seat limits, so not every officer who wants to attend a specific program will be able to do so.[29] Thus, mechanisms exist for obtaining information about which DE program an officer and their senior raters wish for them to attend (i.e., dream sheets) and mechanisms to make the final decision about which officers will attend which programs. The largest programs are ACSC for IDE and AWC for SDE. If an officer does not wish to attend another specific program or is not selected to attend another specific program, he or she will attend ACSC (IDE) or AWC (SDE).

The DEDB at AFPC makes specific decisions about which officers will go to which programs. AFPC is the primary decisionmaker, taking into account recommendations from the DTs. DTs provide two to three school vectors (i.e., recommended schools) for each officer, and

---

[26] One modification in Air Force policy that was discussed while this research was in progress and was made after the research in this report was completed was to create a central PME board to create a rank order of all officers nominated for in-residence schooling by their senior rater. Because this rank order now determines which candidate officers will attend DE in-residence, the role of DTs in making DE decisions now focuses on recommending which in-residence school an officer should attend.

[27] Sometimes, perhaps because of current assignments, it is not possible for an officer to leave for in-residence schooling in the upcoming year. We use *feasibility* to capture this possibility.

[28] CSBs use a technique called gray-zone resolution to draw the final line between officers meeting a promotion board who are selected for promotion and those who are not. Promotion boards typically have too many officers to review for it to be practical for all board members to review all officers' records. As a result, promotion boards organize themselves into panels, each reviewing a subset of all the records and setting two cutoff points. Officers above the first cutoff point are selected for promotion. Those who score above the second cutoff point but below the first in each panel fall into a gray zone from which the entire board selects the final officers to be promoted. The same reasons for using a gray-zone resolution to draw the line between those who are and are not selected for promotion apply to promotion board determination of the top 20 percent who are guaranteed in-residence DE.

[29] Many DE schools have a very limited number of seats, with more officers vying for seats than there are seats available. Thus, a decision must be made about who will be chosen to attend each small school. Several options are available for making these decisions. One reviewer noted that a random process (e.g., using a lottery) for breaking ties would undermine officer confidence in the system. It should be clear that we are not recommending a random process, only noting that such options exist, and are fair in the event of real ties. In conversations with the Air Force, it was clear that the Air Force prefers using a central PME board to make these decisions.

AFPC adjudicates by first choosing who will attend the small schools. The remainder will attend ACSC or AWC. This leads us to our next recommendation:

Recommendation 4: The Air Force should change how decisions are made about small school attendees.

To implement this recommendation, AFPC should select one of the following methods to assign numbers used for tie-breaking in deciding who attends which of the small schools:[30]

- a lottery
- line numbers
- a central PME board.

Determining When Officers Will Attend

AFPC analyses suggest that DTs manipulate timing by delaying CSB school selects to wedge in candidates. For example, consider a single school slot that could be filled with either a "first-look" CSB school select or a DT candidate. A DT could choose the candidate to fill the slot, knowing it might be his or her final opportunity to attend in-residence, while the school select would be guaranteed to attend school in the future. The school select's opportunity to attend DE would be delayed, even though he or she was considered more competitive than the candidate. This leads to our next recommendation:

Recommendation 5: The Air Force should make school assignments in such a way that CSB school selects attend school as early as possible.

To accomplish this, DPA should make school assignments in the following order, to send officers to school at their first available opportunity:

- third-look CSB school selects
- first-look CSB school selects (to fill first-look quota)
- second-look CSB school selects (to fill second-look quota)
- DT candidates (to fill quotas for requirements).

AFPC will have to calculate the above quotas each year.

Providing Feedback to Officers

A key element of the original vision for DTs was to provide feedback for individual career development. This was intended to remedy the perceived lack of mentoring and personalized feedback and was seen as a crucial for balancing officers' personal career goals against the Air Force's organizational needs. Historical documents proposing the creation of DTs state that written feedback must be provided but do not specify the format, content, or process for providing it (e.g., timing, frequency). Prior to the establishment of DTs, little information was

---

[30] The major point here is that ties need to be broken in deciding who attends which small school. If true differences between individuals can be efficiently ascertained, then a central PME board is the most desirable option.

available that compared an officer's performance with that of his or her peers in the career field. As part of the DTs, a cross-section of senior officers from within a career field—its leaders— now review and separately rank the majors and lieutenant colonels in the career field. This is very powerful information and, understandably, must be treated very carefully but could be used for identifying high-potential officers in a career field.

DTs provide required generic guidance, but individual career feedback is generally not provided. DTs routinely provide multiple forms of feedback, some of which directly reflects AF/A1 guidance. DTs provide feedback to senior leaders, commanders, and officers through a variety of mediums (e.g., publishing DT minutes, hosting webinars, emailing officers within the career field directly). The feedback is intended to help officers manage their careers, positioning them for promotion, assignments, and other opportunities. For example, in their published minutes, several DTs highlighted the necessity of checking the accuracy of records to ensure that the board has the most current information available to help with the decisionmaking process. Another item routinely highlighted is to update ADPs; those of many officers are outdated or irrelevant. Of note is that the level of correspondence and feedback to the field differs from DT to DT.

The value of personal feedback leads to the next recommendation:

Recommendation 6: In addition to the feedback they offer the career field at large, DTs should provide personalized feedback to individual officers.

DTs typically provide aggregated feedback to an entire career field, while individual feedback is more sporadic and informal. Officers expressed a great deal of interest in personalized feedback: learning in more depth what DTs thought about their performance. The officers also sought more advice and guidance about what specific opportunities or career moves were considered valuable for the Air Force and, thus, that they should consider for their own career goals. There is evidence to suggest that targeted or personalized feedback is beneficial. For instance, officers who differ in age or expertise may respond differently to feedback and may not benefit equally or similarly from generic feedback. Providing personalized feedback that accounts for these individual differences can result in performance improvements. We recognized that DTs' capability to provide personalized feedback will vary according to their sizes. For large career fields, it is difficult to provide personalized feedback to officers. In such career fields, we suggest that DTs prioritize providing feedback to the identified high-potential officers who may become leaders of their career fields and the corporate Air Force. For example, the officer rankings DTs create could be used to identify the officers career field senior leaders consider to have high potential.

But the kind of feedback officers receive are also important:

Recommendation 7: In providing personalized feedback, DTs should emphasize learning and development.

Research shows that recipients of feedback that is intended (or is perceived to be intended) to guide career development, rather than being merely for administrative purposes (e.g., supervisors using feedback information to influence formal performance appraisals, pay, or promotion opportunities) are more likely to use that feedback constructively, in ways that lead to performance gains (Smither, London, and Reilly, 2005). This may be particularly applicable to DTs: Their broad mandate is to manage overall career development, but in practice, they often determine career opportunities, such as through education and command recommendations. "Personal development plans"—that is, assessment tools for individual career competencies and goals—that are perceived as tools for learning and development lead individuals to increased career development activities and performance (Beausaert et al., 2011). This finding further implies that refining vectors and ODPs to reflect a learning and development orientation is beneficial to the Air Force. Supervisors should therefore make it explicit that the purpose of feedback is forward-looking—that is, for continual learning and development (Beausaert et al., 2011).

Creating Command Lists

Essentially all DTs produce command lists, but DTs do not have a standard way to recommend particular individuals for command. As noted above, one area of potentially conflicting interests between commanders and functional or career fields is in DT's creation of command lists. Some DTs attempt to control the actual assignments to command positions, usurping the commanders' discretion. DT chairs stated that their DTs create command lists either for AFPC to pick or for "commanders to hire commanders," then negotiate and deconflict commanders' picks as needed. These conflicting interests could be balanced by DTs creating command lists that include the DT's clear command assignment recommendations and yet preserve the commanders' prerogatives by providing several recommended individuals from which the commander could choose. Thus,

> **Recommendation 8: The process for managing command lists should be standardized such that DTs provide multiple options for both officers and jobs to avoid pigeonholing officers and jobs.**

Every DT should create a command list. For each officer on the command list, the DT should recommend two to three jobs. Similarly, for each job, multiple—at least three—officers should be recommended. The exact number, however, is not as important as the principle of providing multiple options for both officers and jobs. Because career fields differ in size, not all commanders will have previous knowledge about individual officers within their career fields, and the hiring commander may very often be a member of a different career field. Input from the career field input is therefore important but should be balanced by ensuring that the commander's input is not undeservedly constrained. Providing only one choice for a particular job would force the commander to pick that individual, limiting the commander's options to shape the workforce.

Strategic Objectives for Development Teams

Although we have recommended that vectoring should not be required of the DTs, DTs characteristically engage in wide-ranging discussions of the career fields they are responsible for and of the officers in the career fields. They also characteristically create ranked lists of the officers in their career fields. Taken together, this information essentially identifies the officers the DTs consider to have high potential. The challenge for DTs is that membership changes every year to some degree. Of course, new information may come to light about officers previously considered to have high potential that would change their recommended development path, but without a record of recommended development paths, the following DT loses the benefit of continuity in planning officer development. Thus, we offer a final recommendation:

> **Recommendation 9: All DTs should identify high-potential officers, chart recommended paths for their development, and track their progress.**

Summary

The engagement of senior leaders from each career field in developing their field-grade officers has a number of positive benefits that have convinced us to recommend that DTs continue into the future, with the modifications we have recommended above. In addition, every DT chair we spoke with agreed with us that DTs have substantial value and should continue. The major benefit we see in the DT system is that it requires a broad swath of each career field's senior leaders to take stock of the status of the career field, not just of the numbers in its pipeline but also of the quality of the personnel in that pipeline and the development needs of the career field and of individuals within the career field. With this knowledge in hand, the DTs proceed to make decisions about and provide directions for the development of career field members. Our recommendations are intended to improve DT decisionmaking and to rebalance the system to better support the needs of its major stakeholders.

Appendix A. Interview Protocol

1. What is your role in the process and activities of the Developmental Teams (DTs)?
2. How long have you been in this role?
3. What are primary objectives of the DTs?
4. Do DTs have any other objectives?

   a. What they are?

5. How do DTs go about achieving these objectives?
6. Do DTs affect any other aspects of force development beyond these objectives?
7. Do DTs use any metrics to assess their effectiveness?

   a. May we have access to these metrics?

8. What do these metrics show about the effectiveness of DTs?

Appendix B. 2011 A1 Guidance Memorandum to Development Teams

DEPARTMENT OF THE AIR FORCE
HEADQUARTERS UNITED STATES AIR FORCE
WASHINGTON DC

MEMORANDUM FOR FUNCTIONAL MANAGERS AND DEVELOPMENT TEAM CHAIRS

AUG 0 9 2011

FROM: AF/A1

SUBJECT: Annual A1 Guidance to Development Teams (DT)

The AF/A1 is required to provide annual guidance for DT operations, in accordance with AFI 36-2640, Executing Total Force Development. The guidance will assist you in developing fully-qualified mission ready Airmen. Please focus on the following areas during the upcoming DT season.

Why We Conduct DTs

How well you plan for and execute your DT reflects directly on how well your members are prepared for their missions. Several Functional Authorities have opted to establish a Functional Advisory Council (FAC). These FACs are convened separate from the DT and are used to provide strategic-level oversight to their functional communities. Typical topics include viable career paths for their Airmen, developmental opportunities such as fellowships and career broadening, and management of high-potential Airmen. By having these strategic-level discussions beforehand, you and your team are able to focus more on the individual development of your Airmen during the DT.

Transparency

DTs are charged with ensuring opportunities and expectations are transparent by providing appropriate visibility into the DT. While vectors provide for transparency by giving feedback to the members meeting the DT, your minutes are also key to providing feedback. The most transparent DTs utilize their minutes to provide actionable guidance to Airmen regarding expectations and opportunities within their career field. Remember, the template A1 provides is the minimum required to be reported after a DT. We encourage you to add any additional information you deem relevant. In addition, a webinar is required at the conclusion of each DT to communicate the results directly with your career field. The feedback from the field on these webinars has been overwhelmingly positive, and allows your DT to provide immediate information to your community.

Cross-functionality

Last year we addressed the growing need to review cross-functional mission areas (e.g., Nuclear Enterprise, Irregular Warfare, C2 Operations). As such, you are reminded that each functional area and DT needs to consider these cross-functional arenas when conducting your DT. It is equally important for the cross-functional communities to fully articulate their requirements. While cross-functional communities do not conduct their own DTs, they are encouraged to create advisory panels whose members interact with each DT.

Force Management

The Air Force will continue its force management actions in FY11 and into FY12 because we ended FY10 with 2,300 extra officers and retention projections remain high for 2011 and 2012. As the Air Force continues to reduce officers to meet our authorized, funded end strength, we must have the appropriate balance of skills to meet the needs of the current and future fight. One of our newest efforts occurred earlier this year when we instituted the first, formalized non-rated line officer crossflow program. Many of you realize some of our top Air Force and Joint leaders have experience in more than one specialty. Please think beyond your functional community as you identify and vector top-quality officers to develop other skill sets. Likewise, you should care for and develop officers who flow into your functional communities so they get appropriate training and experience for their grade. We formally crossflowed more than 70 officers earlier this year—please deliberately develop them to be the best the Air Force can offer. As a DT, you must be cognizant of all of these efforts because providing the right vector for the right officer at the right time is critical as the Air Force continues to shape the force.

Inspector General Assignments

Over the last several years, the importance of the IG to the effectiveness and efficiency of the overall Air Force mission has been recognized and emphasized by SECAF, CSAF and numerous reports. We are making significant changes to increase wing "whitespace" while ensuring the IG system produces what commanders at all levels need. To achieve this objective, we need high-quality officers assigned to the Air Staff, the Air Force Inspection Agency, MAJCOM IG teams and wing IG billets. CSAF endorsed this need, directed MAJCOM CCs to hand-select MAJCOM IG Team Chiefs, and asked AF/A1 to make several other changes to ensure personnel assigned to the IG meet the high standards required for their positions as direct representatives of the commander. DTs should strongly consider the unique opportunities an IG assignment provides when considering post-developmental education and post-command assignments.

Language, Region, and Culture

As AF global commitments for security cooperation, building partnerships, security force assistance and stability operations continue to expand, COCOMs and the Air Force require greater inventory of language, region and cultural (LRC) capabilities in the force. Excluding Crypto-Linguist and Regional Affairs Strategists, there are 1,520 language-coded billets in 119 different Air Force Specialties today. As Combatant Commands and Numbered Air Forces and MAJCOMs continue to capture valid LRC requirements, the enterprise value of LRC enabled Airmen continues to escalate. In 2009, the Air Force initiated the Language-Enabled Airmen Program (LEAP), in concert with a deliberate force development plan to select, sustain, and manage language-qualified Airmen to fill these requirements. Currently, there are 194 active duty officers in LEAP whose language is being sustained and improved through E-mentor online training and language immersions.

Starting in FY12 and forward, 400 new Lieutenants with language skills will be selected each year to build the requisite force structure to meet mission requirements. The key to LEAP success is the synchronization of development and utilization. Language utilization in an operational environment not only improves mission effectiveness but also improves language performance. DTs should keep in mind the strategic importance of these Airmen and give them priority when vectoring or considering LEAP Airmen for follow-on language assignments, foreign PME, and OCONUS requirements. Putting language qualified Airmen in language-coded positions is a mission imperative. Understanding the force multiplying impact LRC enabled Airmen bring to the fight, language capability was added to the Officer Selection Brief starting in 2011.

Supporting the Contingency Mission with the Air Force's Best Airmen

We must ensure the Airmen filling critical billets in forward deployed AORs have the required skills and experience to ensure success. The AOR is not the place for training these individuals, especially commanders. These positions must be assigned to experienced, trained leaders. Therefore, the criteria for filling these key billets cannot be driven by volunteerism or Short-Tour Return Date. As our responsibilities in Afghanistan continue, this issue is important. Ensure your selection process for key and critical billets enhances mission success and builds on our Joint partnership efforts.

Diversity

As a reminder, the Air Force recognizes diversity as a strategic imperative, and you play a vital role in advancing and maintaining diversity within your functional areas. The Air Force broadly defines diversity as a composite of *individual characteristics*, *experiences*, and *abilities* consistent with the Air Force Core Values and the Air Force mission. Air Force diversity includes, but is not limited to, *personal life experiences, geographic background, socioeconomic background, cultural knowledge, educational background, work background, language abilities, physical abilities, philosophical/spiritual perspectives, age, race, ethnicity* and *gender*.

Developmental Education Follow-on Assignment Consideration

DTs should make every effort to consider follow-on assignments in conjunction with selection of developmental education opportunities. DTs should consider mandated follow-on assignments with the overall career timing of the individual. Close coordination between DTs and assignment teams will ensure a more deliberate approach to force development. As a reminder, the CJCS focus on Joint Duty has increased and you are reminded of the importance of vectoring only the highest caliber individuals to JDAL billets. The same holds true for Acquisition Corp assignments. If you have members cross flowing or career-broadening into acquisitions, that caliber of person is expected to progress through the promotion ranks at or above rates at which line officers do.

Afghanistan-Pakistan Hands (APH) Program

Effective with the Spring 11 DTs we began an effort to proactively select, track and outplace APH Airmen for this high priority CJCS and AF program. As we are looking for Airmen to spend upwards of 4 years in this program, we need on-going DT involvement to make sure we are selecting the right Airmen. Make sure milestones (Command, IDE/SDE eligibility windows, promotion boards, etc.) are considered for optimum entry and outplacement from the program. As you convene future DTs, there will be an APH segment in your agenda where you will be asked to review all your current Airmen in the APH program to ensure we are taking care of these Airmen. Additionally, we will be asking you to look at APH requirements and vector some of your best and brightest for this high visibility CJCS and AF program. Maintaining a strong "bench" of Airmen to select for future APH requirements will ensure the AF is well represented in this key warfighting program.

Today's Airmen possess an unsurpassed commitment and dedication to service and are a credit to the Joint warfighter and the U.S. Air Force. They enable our competitive advantage against our adversaries and deliver dominance in air, space, and cyberspace. Your efforts to improve and standardize our DTs will have far reaching impact for the future of our Air Force. If you have any force development or DT suggestions for improvement, please don't hesitate to contact my FD shop at afaldi.workflow@pentagon.af.mil.

DARRELL D. JONES
Lieutenant General
DCS, Manpower, Personnel and Services

cc:
Functional Authorities
AFPC/CC
MAJCOM/A1s

Appendix C. Development Team Responsibilities

According to AFI 36-2640, DTs have the following responsibilities:

3.5.1. DTs will identify the education, training, and experiences appropriate for officers and DAF [Department of the Air Force] civilian equivalents within each functional community based on current and future requirements. This includes education and training opportunities funded by the USAF or pursued as self-development by officers and DAF civilians. DTs will provide feedback to CFMs [career field managers]/CFTs [career field teams] to update career field pyramid(s) as necessary.

3.5.2. DTs will understand career field policies, plans, programs, training, and actions affecting career field management and development and will take these issues into consideration when making personnel decisions and vectors.

3.5.3. Each DT meeting will begin with an overview of existing and projected requirements, to include 365-day existing deployment opportunities and existing and projected authorized strength.

3.5.4. DTs will make vectors based on projected/anticipated, aggregated requirements by level and position type. A vector is the DT's collective recommendation for an experience level (e.g., Joint Staff, Air Staff, MAJCOM, base-level, etc.). training or education opportunity (e.g., resident DE, advanced functional training), or position type (e.g., flight commander, division chief, instructor, special duty, etc.) a member should be considered for in his or her next or subsequent assignments.

3.5.5. DTs will use career planning diagrams (i.e., career development pyramid) to make informed vector recommendations and will assist FMs and CFMs with updating this guidance based on career field dynamics as well as current and projected personnel requirements.

3.5.6. DTs will review career field Air Expeditionary Force posturing and coding to ensure capabilities are visible and properly aligned in the Air Expeditionary Force.

3.5.7. DTs must consider cross-functional developmental and utilization requirements when recommending vectors for their officers and DAF civilians. Cross-functional OPRs [offices of primary responsibility] must identify their requirements to individual CFMs/CFTs NLT [no later than] 30 days prior to each scheduled DT session. DT chairs, CFMs, and ATs [assignment teams]/CFTs must ensure these cross-functional requirements are appropriately addressed during DT sessions.

3.5.8. CFMs will provide DT dates to AFPC/DPAPF NLT 60 days prior to each DT. AF/A1 will post DT dates in the respective Officer and Civilian Development Pages on the Air Force Portal.

3.5.9. DTs will provide vector recommendations for DAF civilians selected for career broadening developmental assignments at least one year prior to completion of the program. For example, DAF civilian employees identified for graduation in Fall 2009 will receive a post-broadening vector from the Fall 2008 DT or from an outplacement DT at least one year prior to completion.

3.5.10. DTs will provide vector recommendations for DAF civilians selected for resident Developmental Education (DE) programs during their first DT session following the annual public release of DE selections. For example, DAF civilians identified on the Fall 2007 DE announcement (for Academic Year 08/09) will receive a post-school vector from the Spring 2008 DT, or from the Summer 2008 DT, whichever occurs first.

3.5.11. DTs will provide career feedback to officers, civilians, senior raters, and commanders via the automated Airmen Development Plan system or other similar process.

3.5.12. DTs will use Special Selection panel configuration to determine officer DEDB nominations, Squadron Commander/Director Candidate Lists, BDE [basic developmental education] (AFERB [Air Force Education Requirements Board]–sponsored) programs, Advanced Studies Group nominations, and AF/A1-approved functionally-sponsored development programs. MAJCOM/CVs may request AF/A1 approval to conduct Squadron Commander/Director Special Panel separately from the DT.

3.5.13. Officers who are identified as "selects" for resident DE programs must not be expected to have completed a corresponding non-resident course in order to be recommended for resident DE attendance.

3.5.14. DTs will ensure personnel vectored for Joint duty assignment consideration are of sufficient quality to achieve promotion rates in accordance with joint promotion objectives outlined in Title 10 United States Code, Section 662, *Promotion Policy Objectives for Joint Officers*.

3.5.15. Active component DTs will meet two times per year at a minimum. ARC [Air Reserve Component] DTs will meet as determined by DT Chairs. Specific times will be determined by the FM [functional manager] or Career Field Manager but will fall into standardized windows for the Active component: Fall (October–December); Spring (January–April); and Summer (May–September). Active component DT meetings will be held at AFPC and must be coordinated with AFPC.

References

AFDD—*See* Air Force doctrine document.

AFI—*See* Air Force instruction.

AFPC—*See* Air Force Personnel Center.

AFPD—*See* Air Force policy directive.

Air Force Doctrine Document 1-1, *Leadership and Force Development*, November 8, 2011.

Air Force Instruction 36-2501, *Officer Promotions and Selective Continuation*, Washington, D.C.: Headquarters, Department of the Air Force, July 16, 2004.

Air Force Instruction 36-2640, *Executing Total Force Development*, Washington, D.C.: Headquarters, Department of the Air Force, December 16, 2008.

Air Force Instruction 36-2110, *Assignments*, Washington, D.C. Headquarters, Department of the Air Force, September 22, 2009.

Air Force Instruction 36-3701, *Space Professional Development Program*, Washington, D.C.: Headquarters, Department of the Air Force, May 20, 2010.

Air Force Personnel Center, "Development Team Analysis," briefing, AFPC/DPAP (Defense Procurement and Acquisition Policy), 2012a.

———, "CY12 Intermediate/Senior Developmental Education Board Nomination Procedural Message and Civilian Developmental Education and Civilian Strategic Leader Nomination Call," memorandum for all FSSs, A1s, & J1s, Randolph Air Force Base, Tex.: Headquarters, Air Force Personnel Center, PSDM 12-13, March 1, 2012b.

Air Force Policy Directive 36-26, *Total Force Development*, Washington, D.C.: Headquarters, Department of the Air Force, September 27, 2011.

Beausaert, Simon A. J., Mien S. R. Segers, and Wim H. Gijselaers, "Using a Personal Development Plan for Different Purposes: Its Influence on Undertaking Learning Activities and Job Performance," *Vocations and Learning,* Vol. 4, No. 3, 2011, pp. 231–252.

Callander, Bruce D., "The New Way of Officer Assignments," *Air Force Magazine*, June 1998, pp. 64–67.

Galway, Lionel A., Richard J. Buddin, Michael R. Thirtle, Peter S. H. Ellis, and Judith D. Mele, *Understrength Air Force Officer Career Fields: A Force Management Approach*, Santa Monica, Calif.: RAND Corporation, MG-131-AF, 2005. As of October 31, 2013: http://www.rand.org/pubs/monographs/MG131.html

Hassan, Rich, "Policy Brief: Force Development," September 27, 2002.

Jones, Darrell D., "Memorandum for Functional Managers and Development Team Chairs: Annual A1 Guidance to Development Teams (DT)," Washington, D.C.: Headquarters, U.S. Air Force, August 9, 2011.

———, "Memorandum for Functional Managers and Development Team Chairs: Force Development Guidance," Washington, D.C.: Headquarters, U.S. Air Force, 2012.

McKey, George, "Developmental Education Designation Process," briefing, Air Force Personnel Center, 2012.

McMahan, Michael C., "Officer Professional Development Campaign Plan for the 21st Century," briefing to the Secretary of the Air Force and Chief of Staff of the Air Force, September 18, 2002.

Moore, S. Craig, and Marygail K. Brauner, *Advancing the U.S. Air Force's Force-Development Initiative*, Santa Monica, Calif.: RAND Corporation, MG-545-AF, 2007. As of October 31, 2013:
http://www.rand.org/pubs/monographs/MG545.html

Moore, S. Craig, Brent Thomas, and Raymond E. Conley, *Targeting the Occupational Skill Pairings Needed in New Air Force Colonels*, Santa Monica, Calif.: RAND Corporation, TR-759-AF, 2010. As of December 12, 2014:
http://www.rand.org/pubs/technical_reports/TR759.html

Near, Chris, and David Levin, "United States Air Force Development Teams 2011 Officer Experience and Satisfaction Survey," briefing, Logistics Management Institute, November 2011.

O'Neill, Kevin, *Sustaining the U.S. Air Force's Force Support Career Field Through Officer Workforce Planning*, Santa Monica, Calif.: RAND Corporation, RGSD-302, 2012. As of October 31, 2013:
http://www.rand.org/pubs/rgs_dissertations/RGSD302.html

Robbert, Albert A., Steve Drezner, John E. Boon, Jr., Lawrence M. Hanser, S. Craig Moore, Lynn M. Scott, and Herbert J. Shukiar, *Integrated Planning for the Air Force Senior Leader Workforce*, Santa Monica, Calif.: RAND Corporation, TR-175-AF, 2004. As of December 12, 2014:
http://www.rand.org/pubs/technical_reports/TR175.html

Scott, Lynn M., Raymond E. Conley, Richard Mesic, Edward O'Connell, and Darren D. Medlin, *Human Capital Management for the USAF Cyber Force*, Santa Monica, Calif.: RAND Corporation, DB-579-AF, 2010. As of October 31, 2013:
http://www.rand.org/pubs/documented_briefings/DB579.html

Sitterly, Daniel, "Q&A: Daniel Sitterly," *Military Advanced Education*, Vol. 6, No. 8, October 2011. As of December 17, 2014:
http://www.kmimediagroup.com/military-advanced-education/articles/352-military-advanced-education/mae-2011-volume-6-issue-8-october/4755-qaa-daniel-sitterly-sp-477

Smither, James W., Manuel London, and Richard R. Reilly, "Does Performance Improve Following Multisource Feedback? A Theoretical Model, Meta-Analysis, And Review Of Empirical Findings," *Personnel Psychology,* Vol. 58, No. 1, 2005, pp. 33–66.

Stewart, Alfred, "Memorandum for CAF Development Team Members: Development Team (DT) Welcome Letter," San Antonio, Tex.: Department of the Air Force, Headquarters, Air Force Personnel Center, 2012.

U.S. Air Force, "Policy Brief: Officer Professional Development Campaign Plan for the 21st Century," annotated draft, September 26, 2002.